THE TREATMENT TECHNIQUES OF
HARRY STACK SULLIVAN

The Treatment Techniques of Harry Stack Sullivan

by

A. H. CHAPMAN, M.D.

Visiting Lecturer, The Greater Kansas City Mental Health Foundation. Formerly, Associate Clinical Professor of Psychiatry, University of Kansas School of Medicine, and Attending Psychiatrist, St. Mary's Hospital, Menorah Medical Center and Research Hospital and Medical Center, Kansas City, Missouri

BRUNNER/MAZEL, Publishers • New York

Library of Congress Cataloging in Publication Data

Chapman, Arthur Harry, 1924-
    The treatment techniques of Harry Stack Sullivan.
    Bibliography: p.
    Includes index.

    1. Psychoanalysis.   2. Sullivan, Harry Stack, 1892-1949.   I. Title.
[DNLM: 1. Psychotherapy.   WM420 C466t]
RC506.C47   616.8'917   77-26633
ISBN 0-87630-158-8

Copyright © 1978 by A. H. Chapman

Published by
BRUNNER/MAZEL, INC.
19 Union Square, New York, N.Y. 10003

MANUFACTURED IN THE UNITED STATES OF AMERICA

To the memory of a gifted, generous teacher,

Louis H. Cohen

Late Clinical Professor of Psychiatry, Yale University

and for

Frederico Almeida

Preface

Harry Stack Sullivan is now generally recognized as the most important American-born psychiatrist. So pervasive, and so often unrecognized, is his influence that Leston Havens of the Harvard Medical School has said that he "almost secretly" dominates American psychiatry. This volume is designed to help psychiatrists, clinical psychologists, psychiatric social workers, psychiatric nurses and other mental health professional workers to use Sullivan's techniques in aiding people who have problems in living.

Sullivan views the therapist as a diligent *participant observer* in a vibrant dialogue with the patient. Psychotherapy proceeds through exploring the patient's current and past interpersonal relationships, formulating and testing hypotheses about the patient's difficulties, resolving anxiety in its many forms, and investigating distortions in the patient-therapist relationship. Therapy is an interpersonal process in which one person is recognized as having expert knowledge about interpersonal relationships and emotional functioning and the other person is seeking help for problems in these areas.

In his coverage of psychotherapy, Sullivan does not talk in vague generalities. He quickly gets down to explicit details about what the therapist says and does. He illustrates with precise examples the use of comments and questions in increasing the patient's awareness about himself and his life. He deals with ways for overcoming, and using, the many obstacles that prevent the patient from becoming aware of painful facets of his/her relationships with people. He emphasizes time economy in interviewing; each session should be a useful experience for the patient.

Since language and nonverbal communication are the therapist's two main tools, Sullivan scrutinizes them at length. In his far-ranging discussions of psychotherapy, he considers such diverse subjects as the management of deteriorating communication in the interview, the examination of the patient's future as an area for psychotherapeutic work, manifold ways for decreasing anxiety to keep the therapeutic dialogue vital and relevant, the modifications necessary in doing brief psychotherapy, and many other topics. He describes minutely the conduct of an interview from the therapist's first words in greeting a patient to his final comments at its end.

If American psychotherapy is frankly viewed, it is clear that most therapists spend much time doing some form of Sullivanian therapy, though many of them are only vaguely aware of it. This volume aims at helping them do it better.

The material in these pages comes from a broad range of sources. It relies heavily, of course, on Sullivan's published works. It also uses much material which I have been collecting since 1948; this includes unpublished typed transcriptions of lectures and seminars Sullivan gave, notes taken by various persons at his teaching sessions, oral and written accounts of his viewpoints by people who studied under him at diverse times during the last 15 years of his life, a small amount of material which Sullivan wrote but never published, and other data. Sullivan's viewpoints presented here are those of the last six years of his life. As explained in my book *Harry*

Stack Sullivan: His Life and His Work, Sullivan spent a long time maturing, both as a person and as a psychiatrist; only the teaching sessions, seminars, lectures and writings of his last few years can be accepted as definitive statements of his ideas and treatment techniques. He so extensively modified all his previous views that they must be considered only as preliminary versions of his final formulations.

A book on psychotherapeutic methods acquires clarity by giving brief dialogues to illustrate many aspects of it. Unfortunately there are neither recordings nor verbatim accounts of Sullivan doing psychotherapy in his mature years. I have therefore included many short, illustrative dialogues to explain important points. All too often the reader of a work on psychotherapy asks, "Yes, but how do I put these principles into words when I have a patient in front of me?" For ease and clearness of presentation, these dialogues are more condensed than they would be in actual practice; also, the language tends to be more explicit and terse. However, they accurately demonstrate the techniques involved and furnish examples of Sullivan's methods.

The outlines of Sullivan's theories which are given in these pages and which accompany each dialogue make this volume self-sufficient. However, readers who want to know more about Sullivan's concepts should go on to read some of his works which are discussed in Chapter 11.

The persistent question which Sullivan asks is, "How *useful* is this in helping patients?" The answers he presents can aid therapists of all orientations to deal more effectively with the opportunities and challenges they constantly encounter in psychotherapeutic work.

A. H. CHAPMAN

Contents

THE TREATMENT TECHNIQUES OF
HARRY STACK SULLIVAN

Chapter 1

The Things a Therapist Does and Says in an Interview: Participant Observation

INTERPERSONAL PSYCHOTHERAPY

In psychotherapy two persons enter into a joint venture to try to solve the problems in living of one of them. One of these persons is designated the therapist, and he or she assumes the role of an expert in interpersonal relationships and emotional functioning. The other is designated the patient, or client, and he or she has one or many problems in living for which he is seeking help.

A dialogue, involving both verbal and nonverbal interchanges, occurs. In interpersonal therapy this dialogue is an alert, brisk process involving long and short stretches of talk by the patient, and comments, questions and short statements by the therapist. The therapist is not an aloof, detached observer who occasionally makes interpretations; he is an active *participant* in the ongoing process which he is *observing*. He uses his personality and special skills to help the patient. The role and activities of the therapist are summarized in the term *participant observation*.

Sullivan feels that the concept of an aloof, uninvolved thera-

1

pist who holds up a mirror to the patient to see his problems, or who acts as a screen onto which the patient projects his disturbed ways of relating to people, is not possible. From the first moment of the initial interview the therapist, by his words, acts and stances, greatly affects the course of the therapeutic process. Regardless of how much or little he says, the therapist influences what the patient says and the kinds of material he deals with. The therapist's behavior has a decided effect on the type of relationship that arises between him and the patient.

The term most often used in designating Sullivan's methods of therapy is *interpersonal psychotherapy*. This term emphasizes that psychotherapy always is an ongoing *interpersonal* process between two people; in group therapy, hospital ward milieu therapy and some other types of treatment more than two persons are, of course, involved. Sullivan was the first mental health professional worker to use the word *interpersonal* basically in his thinking, and to build his treatment methods and theories on interpersonal relationships. *Interpersonal* is as specific for Sullivan as *psychoanalytic* is for Freud.

In some instances a therapist should define these things to a patient. Some therapists assume that patients know what they are supposed to do in therapy and understand what the therapist's functions are. A well informed minority of patients do know these things. Many other patients do not, or they have incorrect ideas gleaned from television programs, sensationalist movies and misleading popular books.

In interpersonal psychotherapy the therapist tries to make all things clear in brief, simple statements. *He takes nothing for granted.* Sullivan repeatedly urges: *Do not assume you know what the patient is talking about. You don't know until you find out by engaging in an active dialogue in which you test each hypothesis and check each fact.*

An important corollary of this is: *Do not assume that the patient understands what you are talking about until you make sure in an alert dialogue.* This dialogue involves comments, questions, answers and brief explanations.

Psychotherapy is a highly individualized process. No two therapists do it in exactly the same way, and the problems of no two patients are identical. The following dialogue illustrates how the ideas outlined above can be handled in psychotherapy. At some time in the first few interviews the following interchange may occur. As pointed out in the preface, for purposes of clarity the illustrative dialogues used in this book tend to be more concise and exact in language than often is the case in actual therapy.

Therapist: At this point we perhaps should make clear what we are trying to do. How do you see therapy?

Patient: Well, I'm trying to get over my tenseness and to solve some of my marital problems.

Therapist: Yes, to put it in slightly different terms, we're trying to help you be more comfortable and to do better in your relationships with people. How do you see the ways we're attempting to do these things?

Patient: We talk about my problems. I guess I do most of of the talking.

Therapist: Right, and the more spontaneous you can be, the better. How do you see my role?

Patient: You point out what my troubles are and what to do about them.

Therapist: To some extent, yes. My role is to try to be an expert on problems in living. By questions and comments I try to help you in talking about your difficulties, and to see them in new ways.

Patient: Are you going to analyze me?

Therapist: No, you and I are engaged in a *joint* exploration into what is going on in your life and what has gone on in it. We examine these things and work on them. I shall never *tell you* what is wrong with you. We shall try to *find out together*.

In this brief interchange the therapist has made sure that he and the patient have a clear idea about what they are doing. The therapist can be certain of this only after he and the patient have covered it in a distinct manner.

THE DIRECTION OF THERAPY

The therapist never knows precisely where he and the patient are going. Beyond a few sessions into the future, and sometimes not that far, the therapist cannot foresee what the course of therapy will be. This flexibility and lack of dogmatism about the direction of therapy are a central feature of interpersonal psychotherapy.

The therapist does not assume from the nature of the patient's difficulties what his life history has been. For example, he does not assume that because a patient has an obsessive compulsive problem he suffered a fairly predictable kind of emotional trauma at a specific period in his earlier life. The patient's symptoms and general personality difficulties do not identify the types of interpersonal traumas that have made him the sort of person he is. Moreover, they do not indicate the kind of relationship the patient will set up with the therapist, nor do they determine in a foreseeable manner how he will behave in treatment.

Sullivan feels that when a therapist assumes that he more or less knows what has gone on in the patient's life to produce the kinds of emotional problems he has, he tends to collect from the patient information that confirms his prejudices. The therapist overlooks some data, emphasizes other information and pieces together fragments of the patient's experience in ways that justify his theories. A therapist should participate in therapy with an entirely open mind about what he and the patient may discover.

This sometimes should be made clear to patients.

Patient: Perhaps you can tell me what to expect in treatment and what we shall probably talk about.

Therapist: Could you tell me a little more about what you mean by that question?

Patient: Well, what should I talk about? Should we go back to my childhood? What are we looking for? What sorts of things in a person's life usually cause troubles like mine?

Therapist: When we know the answers to those questions, therapy will be over. I can't tell you what has happened in your life. We must find out together. Your symptoms and the kinds of difficulties you have in getting along with people do not tell us what has gone wrong in your life. Each person's life is too individual to allow that.

Patient: Then how do we find out?

Therapist: We explore your life and your relationships with people, past and present, by talking about them. We don't know what the next hour, or even perhaps the next minute, will reveal. The important thing is that we constantly deal with things, big and small, that are significant to you.

THE THERAPIST'S BASIC ATTITUDES

The therapist should have a rapt, concentrated interest in the patient and a sincere desire to help and understand him. In addition, he should have a profound respect for the patient; he should feel that his problems are well worth solving. An aloof, or coldly objective, or bored, or uninterested therapist is unlikely to help people. The therapist is not a scientist studying the patient as an interesting specimen; he is a fellow human being who has special training to aid him in solving his problems in living.

However, despite his marked interest in the patient and his respect for him, the therapist does not expect in the treatment relationship any of the usual gratifications of interpersonal life. He does not seek prestige, nor friendship, nor gratitude nor any of the other satisfactions that may come from relationships with people. His only satisfactions are those of a craftsman who is using his utmost competence in the work at hand, and in being adequately paid for his work. The therapist's main reward is the pleasure of doing a good job in a kind of work that requires skill and attentiveness. However, the therapist never tries to impress the patient with his astuteness and devotion to his task; he merely does what he is trained to do. A therapist who seeks more than this has problems of his own to solve, and until they are solved they will to some extent hamper him.

This must sometimes be defined.

Patient: I'm grateful for the progress I've made, and I appreciate what you've done for me.

Therapist: These gains have been made by *us*, not *me*. *You* have done most of the work. As a therapist, I have only tried to be as skillful as I can be.

Patient: I couldn't have done it alone. You've helped me a lot.

Therapist: We have worked together. I'm glad you're better; it means that our work is succeeding. Our job is to make sense of your life and problems, and the importance of this task pushes aside all other considerations and feelings. In going on with this work, perhaps we might consider other aspects of how your relationship with your husband has. . . .

FUNDAMENTAL PROCEDURES

Psychotherapy as a rule begins with simple events and later proceeds to examine general issues. It starts with commonplace things.

This is illustrated in the following interchange.

Patient: One of my main problems is my passivity.

Therapist: Let's find out what you mean by passivity. Can you give me an example of a situation in which you were passive?

Patient: Today at work Mr. Parker shoved a report onto me that he should write.

Therapist: Does he often do this?

The therapist here has moved therapy from consideration of an abstract thing called the patient's *passivity* to examination of an interpersonal event. Few people can solve emotional problems by discussing them in abstract, general terms; they must examine concrete things that are going on, and have gone on, in their lives.

The techniques of communication employed in psychotherapy are no different from those used in other interpersonal situations. Treatment proceeds by periods of talk, comments, questions and brief explanations. Short, clear words are better than long, obscure ones. *Everything should, if possible, be put in terms of relationships between people.* The following brief exchange illustrates this.

Patient: I think I've made progress in working on my passivity.

Therapist: I agree. You are now able to stick up for yourself and to be firm with people more comfortably.

In this simple exchange the therapist has shifted attention from "passivity," which is vague and could mean many things, to the patient's ability "to stick up for himself" and "to be firm with people"; these are clearly understood *interpersonal acts*. When patients and therapists talk about "passivity," "aggressiveness," "insecurity," "immaturity" and many other similar attributes they in many instances are not talking about the same thing. They may continue for weeks or months without realizing that each of them means something different by such words. However, when they talk about "sticking up for oneself" and "being firm with people," it is difficult for them to misunderstand each other.

Sullivan emphasizes that since words are important tools in psychotherapy therapists should pay more attention to what they do with them.

A therapist should never assume that he knows what a patient is talking about because the patient's words sound familiar, or seem to make sense, or fit the therapist's theories about the kind of problem the patient has. For example, if a patient says, "I became tense when my mother was hostile to me," the therapist should find out *what the patient means*. This simple statement may mean many things, and the therapist and the patient do not know what they are until they explore them. For example, when the patient says, "I *became* tense," the therapist may inquire what his emotional state was *before* this incident occurred. Was he, in fact, emotionally tense before this happened, or did he become tense only after it? Was he already tense about things in his relationship with his mother, and did this event merely focus his attention on his tenseness?

Moreover, what does the patient mean by the word *tense*? Does he mean apprehensive, or fearful, or guilty, or overwhelmed by feelings of inadequacy? Other things may be important. Did this event occur in the morning when his mother usually was calm, or did it occur after she had had a long and tiring day and at such times tended to be argumentative? Was anything else going on in his mother's life at this time that rendered her chronically irritable? Was her marriage troubled? Was she under economic pressures, or struggling with problems at her job, or embroiled in a painful relationship with her own mother?

The therapist does not know the answers to these questions, and, still more important, *he should not assume that the patient does*. If the patient were the kind of person who knew these things and had assimilated them comfortably, he probably would not have the difficulties that are causing him to see a therapist.

Sullivan points out that many therapists let large amounts of important material go by without looking into it, and this material may be lost permanently to both the patient and the therapist. *Finding these things out and assimilating them, in the broadest sense of these words, are what help the patient get well.*

Sullivan puts emphasis on the difference between *speculating* and *knowing*. Each speculation must be investigated and tested to see if it is true. For instance, as the patient and the therapist in this case discuss the mother's hostility, the therapist may begin to speculate that she was not hostile at all. This speculation must be tested by detailed inquiry. It may be revealed that in her alleged hostility she collapsed tearfully into a chair and said, "You've done it again." Exploration of this may show that, rather than feeling hostility, she felt inadequacy as a mother in rearing her son, or panic about various failures in family relationships or fear of the patient's acts. The therapist's speculation that the mother's predominant feeling was something other than hostility becomes secure knowledge as he and the patient investigate all circumstances about it. This opens new areas for the patient and the therapist to examine. Many things the patient has never grasped are now available for comprehension and assimilation.

Furthermore, if his mother's dominant feeling in this incident was not hostility, why did the patient use this word? Was hostility an easier thing for him to come to grips with than his mother's actual feelings? Was he particularly sensitive to anger and depreciation of other people toward him, and did he tend to interpret most upset feelings of others toward him as hostility? Was "hostile" merely an easy jargon word that he latched onto?

The areas for investigation thus spread out more widely and more deeply. Therapy proceeds by exploring them in a vibrant dialogue. This requires intense concentration and much hard work by the therapist. Sullivan states that the therapist who sits back and lets the patient talk without detailed investigation of what he is saying lets 90 per cent of the important material escape. He and the patient rarely come *to a well verified conclusion about anything.*

In this work, elaborate theoretical structures are avoided. The therapist who approaches the patient with a complex theoretical framework in mind will have a hard time seeing what is wrong with him. If, as examples, the therapist feels that the problems of this particular kind of patient are always caused by conditioned fears, or sexual conflicts, or unfulfilled unconscious archetypes, or existential dilemmas, or any other specific theoretical problems, the therapist is prone to see only the things that tend to support his theories and to overlook the other aspects of the patient's life. Sullivan views intricate theories and profuse terminology as stumbling blocks in coming to grips with the patient's true problems. The therapist who is highly committed to a particular theoretical system is prone to engage in an intellectual game with the patient and has little chance of discovering and solving his difficulties.

THE USE OF QUESTIONS

In general, questions are more useful than statements in psychotherapy. A patient may brush a statement aside, and let it go by with little reaction. A question, on the other hand, requires an answer; it rivets the patient's attention to the issue at hand. For example, if a therapist states, "Your father was hostile toward you," the patient may ignore it and feel little impact. If, however, the therapist puts the same thing in the form of a question, "Was your father often so hostile toward you?" the patient's attention is forcibly directed to this point; he is required to make an answer, or at least an answer is strongly indicated.

A question also opens up new areas for discussion. Thus, if the therapist says, "He was angered by what you said," no clear directions for further consideration are offered. If, however, the therapist asks, "Why do you think he was so angered by what you said?" a new channel for investigation is indicated. The interview acquires fresh vitality.

Sullivan frequently stresses the usefulness of the inquiry, "What do you mean by that?" The therapist's voice tone is, of course, important. Nonverbal factors also may be significant. For example, by a slight concentration in facial expression and a gentle tilting of the head the therapist indicates a sympathetic interest in comprehending more clearly what the patient is trying to say. By a mild emphasis on the word *mean* he demonstrates that he is not challenging what the patient is saying, but is merely trying to understand it better for the mutual benefit of both of them.

At other times the therapist may employ the same question to express tactful unwillingness to accept the unreality of a delusional or grossly erroneous statement. In this case he puts the emphasis on the word *that*. If, for example, the patient says that his neighbors are tapping his telephone wires, the therapist responds in a tone of mild incredulity, "What do you mean by *that*?" The therapist, of course, does not argue with the patient about his delusional belief; it usually is a mistake to express blunt nonacceptance of a delusional idea. Nevertheless, a therapist on many occasions should show that he cannot share this belief with the patient and is open to examining why the patient thinks such a thing. The therapist thus can represent reality to the patient without endangering the patient-therapist relationship by outright rejection of the patient's words.

In yet another variation of the same question, the therapist may use his vocal intonation to represent reality to the patient and open a subject for active inquiry. For instance, if an anxious adolescent says that he sometimes feels people can tell by the bags under his eyes that he masturbates, the therapist may ask, "*What* do you mean by that?"

A question frequently should be buffered by an introductory statement. For instance, the therapist may say, "I can see why it looks that way to you, but. . . ." Having in this way reassured the patient that his viewpoint is neither ridiculous nor obviously unjustified, the therapist can explore the meaning, and perhaps test the validity, of what the patient said. Thus, he may say, "I can see why it looks that way to you, but do others also feel he tries to dominate you?" or "I can see why it seems that way, but do others say things that confirm your viewpoint about it?"

The therapist sometimes uses questions to put gentle pressure on a patient to defend his viewpoint; he does this especially with patients who feel they are inferior, inadequate, loathsome or guilty. "Now tell me, what did you ever do that causes you to have such a low opinion of yourself?" "What makes you think that these homosexual episodes were so terrible?" In succeeding inquiries, which may continue for the rest of the interview and extend into later ones, attention is fixed on the details of the experiences being discussed. "Did your mother think you were the only person who ever did poorly for a couple of years in grade school?" "Just who was damaged by these brief homosexual experiences? How common do you think such encounters are between 12-year-old boys?" Such questions explore content, resolve anxiety and open new regions for examination.

The therapist often asks questions because he does not understand what is going on, and he may frankly say so. "I don't understand. Let's take a look at this more closely. When she said that you. . . ." "I'm not clear about what exactly occurred. Do you feel he came to your apartment with the intention of. . . ." By his facial expression and voice tone the therapist conveys sincere doubt. He avoids giving the impression that the patient has expressed himself poorly or has erred in his interpretation of what went on. The therapist may underline this by a preliminary statement. "Incidents of this kind often are difficult to untangle and understand. I'm not sure about this. When she said that you. . . ."

The therapist sometimes can clarify a point for both himself and the patient by crystallizing it in a question that uses new words. "Putting the matter in other words, do you mean that he wanted you to give in to him on this issue?" In such instances he often makes vague things concrete and substitutes short words for long, imprecise ones. "If we face this frankly, do you mean that you felt dirty and worthless afterward?" The therapist asks such questions in ways that illuminate issues and reduce anxiety; he is careful not to undermine the patient's self-esteem with them.

Sullivan feels that questions as a rule are more useful than statements in making a patient's feelings clear to him. This is in keeping with Sullivan's thesis that *you do not tell a patient what is wrong with him, but with him jointly explore what his trouble is.* "Did you feel *afraid* when that happened?" "Did that make you feel *guilty*?" In each case the question should refer to a specific interpersonal event. It is better to ask, "Did you feel guilty when your father said that to you after you did it?" than to say, "Did you often feel guilty when you were a boy?" A person's feelings have much more significance to him when they are related to particular interpersonal incidents rather than to abstract, general issues.

There are, of course, exceptions to these general rules. The therapist, for example, should use *safe questions* with patients who are easily made anxious by probing. Strong anxiety makes it difficult for a patient to talk in useful ways, and panic often destroys an interview situation. Thus, with an easily upset patient it may be better to ask, "How did she annoy you?" than "Did her angry tirades make you feel worthless?" It may be desirable to ask a safe question such as "What happened after that?" rather than "Was it after this argument that she made her suicidal attempt?" Safe questions in many cases allow the patient to determine whether a topic is too anxiety-ridden to discuss at that time. After observing the patient's reactions to a few safe questions, the therapist can decide whether to pursue the subject or to shift attention to another area for the time being.

The therapist frequently uses *indirect questions*. An indirect question seeks information whose eventual object is not at once apparent. In contrast, a *direct question* strikes immediately at the point in question.

In many cases indirect questions elicit more information than direct ones. Indirect questions also focus attention on *interpersonal* aspects of the problem at hand. For example, in a *direct question* the therapist might ask, "Was your mother a fearful person?" Though this may be an advisable question in some instances, *it does not focus attention on specific incidents* and *it does not put the matter in interpersonal terms* (by *interpersonal terms* we mean an event in which two or more people are involved).

Indirect questions, pursuing the same information, would put matter in interpersonal terms and would focus on specific incidents, as follows. "Was your mother afraid of arousing irritability in other people?" "Was she timid in approaching people whom she did not know well?" "As a child, did your temper tantrums seem to frighten her?" By these *indirect* questions the therapist gradually is getting information about whether the mother was a fearful person, and each bit of information is related to a particular kind of interpersonal relationship.

Indirect questions also allow the therapist to proceed cautiously in exploring a topic. He can withdraw from it or shift to another area if the topic appears too painful for the patient to tolerate at that time. This is illustrated in the following dialogue.

Therapist: During your last year in grade school, did you and Bob get to know each other pretty well?

Patient: Yes, he was my best friend. I guess you'd say we were pretty close.

Therapist: What sorts of things did you and he do together?

Patient: Lots of things. We spent a lot of time watching television together in the afternoons. Sometimes we watched it at my house and sometimes at his house, and once in a while we made ourselves hamburgers and milk shakes and ate them while watching TV.

Therapist: Was your mother, or his mother around when you did this?

Patient: Usually not. His mother worked, and my mother went out a lot in the afternoons.

Therapist: Then were you and Bob alone together in the

house much of the time when you were watching television?

Patient: (Growing restless) I guess so. (He rambles for a couple of minutes on unrelated topics.)

Therapist: In which room of your house, and Bob's house, did you usually watch television?

Patient: (Becoming visibly anxious) Well, it was usually in the family room, but sometimes we took a portable TV set to his bedroom or to mine, and watched it there, I guess. . . .

The therapist is using indirect questions to explore cautiously whether a homosexual relationship sprang up between the patient and Bob, who was four years older than him. The patient's increasing agitation as the details of his relationship with Bob are examined may cause the therapist to feel that this area is too anxiety-ridden to investigate at this time, and he may direct the interview into another facet of the patient's life. A direct question such as "Did you and Bob have any homosexual activities?" might arouse so much anxiety that the interview would become seriously hampered. In some cases injudicious direct questions may make the treatment so painful that the patient abandons it altogether.

Indirect questions have another field of usefulness. They may allow the therapist and the patient to discuss a painful subject without undermining the patient's self-esteem. Sullivan uses the term *self-esteem* as a technical word to designate all the things that make a person feel he is a worthwhile human being. It encompasses an individual's feelings of value as a person and competence in interpersonal dealings.

The patient's self-esteem should not be assailed in psychotherapy. Indirect questions frequently are valuable in this respect, as illustrated in the following example. In discussing with a patient a problem she has with her husband, it may be an error to ask, "Have you talked this over with him?" If the patient has not discussed the subject with him, she may feel that the therapist's inquiry implies that she has blundered by not doing so. Indirect questions which do not undermine the patient's self-esteem may be much better. "What does your husband think about this problem? Has he brought the subject up with you? Has he in other ways made his feelings clear on this point? Do you think it would be advisable to get this problem out into the open between the two of you?"

A comment should at this point be made about "loaded questions." A loaded question is one whose answer is strongly influenced by the way in which the question is framed. For example, the question, "Why did you do that hostile thing?" is loaded insofar as it implies that the patient's action *was* hostile. An unloaded, equivalent question would be, "Why did you do that thing?" In this form the question does not imply whether or not the action was hostile. In general, a therapist should use loaded questions *to convey information*, and not to procure it. For example, if, after discussing some act of the patient, the therapist wishes to point out that it was hostile, he may quite properly say, "Why did you do that hostile thing?" Here the therapist is summarizing information already gathered and is preparing the way for new steps.

As mentioned above, Sullivan feels that since words (with their nonverbal accompaniments) are the implements with which therapists work, some attention to their most effective use should be included in teaching psychotherapy. It is an odd fact that most distinguished psychiatric innovators have paid little or no attention to *the precise verbal and nonverbal techniques* that therapists use to obtain and convey information with patients.

TIME ECONOMY IN INTERVIEWING

Sullivan feels that an interview should be a brisk, vibrant process in which time is not wasted; a reasonable amount of work should be done in each session. The therapist does not allow the interview to stagnate on trifles, irrelevant material and unprofitable digressions. When this occurs, the therapist directs attention to more meaningful areas. "Perhaps we might return to considering your feelings at the time of your parents' divorce." "Going back to the period when you were away from home, did you miss anyone in particular?" The therapist, of course, does not censure the patient nor imply that time has been wasted; he simply shifts attention to a more useful area. A change of vocal tone or an alteration of facial expression by the therapist may make this transition smooth.

The therapist avoids irrelevant comments that clog the interview. He does not talk merely to be talking; he does not say, "I see," "I understand," "That's right" and other empty phrases which are meaningless verbal ornaments in the interview. "I see," "I understand" and "Uh huh" do not elicit information, nor give useful directions to therapy, nor open new areas for consideration. They do not make clear *what* the therapist is seeing, or understanding, or supportively agreeing with. These expressions may, of course, occasionally be useful with frightened or hesitant patients, but they should be employed sparingly. As a rule, a more specific statement is better. "I see why you were panicked by that." "I understand why that puzzled you."

A therapist should express himself concisely and clearly, and he should not lecture or nag the patient. He usually can make his point in one to five well phrased sentences. Then he is through. If he goes on longer, he often loses the patient;

the patient stops listening and the impact of what the therapist says loses its force.

Instead of lecturing the patient on any one thing, the same issue is reapproached many times from different points of view. Various similar interpersonal incidents in the patient's life are examined. In each case the therapist makes his comments in a brief, telling manner, and then stops. If the talk of some therapists is studied, it is found that after the first one to five sentences they are simply repeating what they have already said, and this soon resembles scolding.

This is made clear in the two following examples, in which the therapist in essence says the same thing.

1. *Therapist*: Once more you became panicky as you got sexually close to a woman.
2. *Therapist*: As you got close to her you became tense. You felt very uncomfortable as the prospect of sexual intimacy loomed up. Your anxiety built into virtual panic. This is what we have seen happen in previous similar situations which we have discussed during therapy. It occurs whenever the prospect of physical closeness to a woman presents itself. Such closeness frightens you."

Some therapists can pad a one-sentence statement into a several-minute discourse, and frequently do so. Empty lecturing is unproductive. Patients sense that they are being lectured, though they may not be able to put the feeling clearly into words, and it resembles much previous sermonizing they have had from authoritative people such as parents, school officials, vocational supervisors and others. They simply stop listening, since lecturing arouses feelings of hostility, inadequacy, guilt or shame.

Sullivan rarely uses the words *interpret* and *interpretation*. To some extent, this may be a literary habit. However, it has a profounder significance. As mentioned above, Sullivan feels that a therapist should try to avoid telling a patient what is wrong with him; instead, he and the patient engage in a joint effort to discover his difficulties. Sullivan feels that the word *interpret* has an authoritarian ring; instead of *interpret* he employs words like *say, comment, inquire, point out, indicate* and others. This is a small point, but it is worth noting since there is a difference of viewpoint involved.

The therapist should make one point at a time. There is one notable exception to this general rule. It occurs in the formulation, or summary (discussed in Chapter 10), in which the therapist draws a number of points together at the end of an interview, or series of interviews.

If a therapist has several points to make, he does so separately, and he makes each point in reference to a different interpersonal incident. For example, the therapist does *not* say, "Your relationship with your sister was distant and hostile. This hostility was produced by your parents' tendency to play the two of you off against each other. This caused competitiveness and distrust between your sister and yourself. The reasons your parents did this are found in their own personality problems, and also in difficulties between the two of them. Each of them did the same thing in other close relationships in family life and in other situations."

This is too much for a patient to digest at one time. Half a dozen separate points are being made. Each one should be made separately in relation to a specific interpersonal incident. For instance, after discussing a particular interpersonal event, the therapist points out the hostility between the patient and her sister. After examining another interpersonal situation, the therapist shows how the parents played the two girls off against each other. One by one the other points are handled during the course of one or many interviews.

Sullivan rejects the concept that there are indefinitely extensive amounts of therapeutic time in which the patient can explore his problems. He feels that such methods are wasteful and sometimes are counterproductive. He believes that the poor use of time may create barriers to its more concentrated employment later. A patient who has become accustomed to spending large amounts of time in unproductive ways may subsequently resist its more intensive utilization; he tends to cling to a desultory, drifting kind of treatment rather than to engage in the hard work of more concentrated therapeutic effort.

Sullivan emphasizes that doing psychotherapy is hard work; he says it is the hardest work he knows, and he spent his childhood and early adolescence doing manual labor on his father's small farm. He feels that enthusiasm about doing psychotherapy is treacherous and that a therapist who is highly enthusiastic about doing it simply does not understand the intimidating complexity of his job.

Chapter 2

Awareness and Unawareness

AWARENESS

Sullivan's concepts of awareness and unawareness are fundamental in his approach to psychotherapy, and a brief discussion of them is necessary before considering further aspects of his therapeutic methods.

A person is aware of the nature and significance of his experiences in varying degrees. We shall consider the meaning of this statement by applying it to a specific situation.

A college student is typing the notes of a laboratory experiment. After typing several lines she rips the paper from the typewriter, crumples it irritably and throws it in the wastebasket.

On the most superficial level of awareness, this student is aware that she is typing a laboratory experiment report, that she is dissatisfied with what she has written and that she pulls the paper from the typewriter and throws it away. She may be aware of little more than this as she concentrates on her task; all other things lie outside her immediate focus of awareness.

There are many areas of this experience of which this student is unaware, and the ease with which she may become aware of them varies much from one area to another.

On the most elementary level, she is unaware of the thoughts which make her hand muscles move in their precise motions on the typewriter keys. She does not think out the actions of each finger as it goes from key to key. However, at one time she was aware of these things. When several years earlier she was learning to type, she meticulously thought out each of these movements. As she became a proficient typist, these thoughts passed outside her field of awareness; she was then aware only of the literary material she was typing. If necessary, she could, of course, become aware again of the thoughts that propel her fingers over the keyboard; these thoughts are part of her readily available fund of aware experience.

This student is unaware of many more things as she is typing. Some of them are complex and subtle. She performed this laboratory experiment with another student and they quarreled during it. As a result, they are writing their reports separately instead of jointly. This makes her job much more difficult. If asked by her roommate, who is studying in a nearby chair, why she is so irritable, she probably would reply that she is engaged in a difficult, exasperating task. She is *unaware* that much of her vexation is derived from lingering hostility toward the fellow student with whom she quarreled during the experiment, and that this quarrel is causing her much inconvenience and trouble in drawing up the report.

However, this body of feelings and thoughts could easily be brought into her field of awareness. If her roommate said, "You're still upset about the fight you had with John while doing this experiment; your anger is coming out as you write up the report," the student might reflect for a moment and then agree with her. *Her awareness of the determinants of her feelings and actions would thus be enlarged,* and she might become less upset and might do her job more effectively.

There are many other aspects of her behavior about which she is unaware, and she might have much difficulty in becoming aware of them. Throughout her childhood and adolescence she had a hostile relationship with a domineering, cold father; in this relationship she developed a tendency to quarrel with men with whom she is closely associated. She had worked closely with John for an extended period on this laboratory experiment and, after disagreeing over a minor point, she tongue-lashed him. They completed the experiment in sullen coldness. In this incident she carried over into her relationship with John some emotional and interpersonal problems whose origins lie in an earlier period of her life.

The extent to which she could develop awareness of these deeper determinants of her behavior depends on many variables. They include her basic personality structure, the nature of her relationship with the person (such as a friend or a therapist) who was trying to enlarge her awareness, and many other things. If she found awareness of these more painful causes of her behavior very uncomfortable, she might reject them flatly. If, however, such awareness was not too threatening, she might accept it. For instance, if her roommate said, "You always end up fighting with any man you work with; I guess it's a holdover from the lousy relationship you had with your Dad," she would probably reject this statement if it mobilized marked anxiety in her. If, on the other hand, it did not precipitate undue anxiousness, she might recognize some validity in it, or accept it altogether. In the latter case, her awareness would be distinctly enlarged.

There may be many other aspects of this student's feelings and thoughts which are so painful that she could become aware of them only by means of professional psychotherapeutic help. For example, she may have marked feelings of inadequacy which she tends to cover with a veneer of aggressive self-assurance. These feelings may to a large extent be residues of chronic criticism and depreciation by her father. She may lack the capacity for comfortable compromises with men in an easy give-and-take manner, and she may have a deep-seated feeling that all close relationships with men deteriorate into the same kind of painful association she had with her father. Such problems may have contributed to her quarrel with John. To bring these things into her field of comfortable awareness might be a challenging therapeutic task.

Bringing painful unaware things into the patient's field of comfortable awareness is a fundamental aspect of Sullivanian psychotherapy. As will be discussed in the next section, Sullivan does not use the concept of "mind"; hence, transitions of feelings and thoughts from unawareness to awareness have nothing to do with concepts such as the conscious and unconscious minds. Awareness and unawareness are nothing more than qualities of thoughts and feelings. In the same sense that a thought or feeling may be strong or weak, and painful or comfortable, it may be aware or unaware. The ease with which thoughts and feelings can pass from unawareness to awareness, and back again, varies greatly from person to person, and from one time to another in the same person, and from one particular body of thoughts and feelings to another.

A closer inspection of these basic Sullivanian principles will occupy us in the following section.

THE CONCEPT OF "MIND" IN INTERPERSONAL THERAPY

The simple case vignette in the preceding section emphasizes some fundamental differences between Sullivan's interpersonal psychotherapy and other psychiatric systems. Sullivan does not use the concept of the "mind," since he feels that all things said to be lodged in it and to be occurring there cannot be scientifically verified. Statements about the mind and its activities cannot be proved or disproved by objective observations made by any reasonably qualified person. Any system which claims to be scientific must formulate all its principles in ways that allow them to be proved or disproved by objective experiments and observations.

Instead, Sullivan bases his entire system of psychotherapy on interpersonal relationships, since things going on between people in interpersonal relationships can be directly observed. Any adequately trained observer can see, hear and feel what is occurring between two or more people; this opens the way for psychiatry and psychotherapy to evolve into scientific disciplines.

If carefully analyzed, all statements about things said to be occurring in the mind are like the statement "All events are controlled by Divine Providence." This statement is so set up that it can be neither proved nor disproved. Much evidence can be assembled to show that it is so, and much evidence can be marshaled to demonstrate that it is not so, but it can never be proved true or untrue. It must forever remain a matter of speculation or faith. This places it beyond the reach of science, since science requires that all propositions are in time capable of proof or disproof.

A psychiatric system built on elaborate concepts of the structure and functions of the mind can be used to "explain" everything if the system is sufficiently intricate and flexible; the proponents of such a system can claim that much evidence "corroborates" it. However, an indefinitely large number of other systems can be built which also portray the structure and functions of the mind in completely different ways, and they too can "explain" everything if they are sufficiently intricate and flexible. Much of this has been done in psychiatry during the twentieth century and it is one of the main causes of the current disarray in psychiatry and psycho-therapy.

This situation has a historical explanation. In the last years of the nineteenth century and in the early decades of the current one many psychiatrists, psychologists and other behavioral scientists carried the concept of "mind" from philosophy, religion and popular beliefs over into psychiatry, psychology and allied mental health fields. The concept of "mind" is quite acceptable in philosophy, religion and popular belief since these bodies of thought do not require that all their principles be set up in ways that make them subject to proof or disproof by objective scientific experiments and observations.

Herein lies one of the truly revolutionary qualities of Sullivan's viewpoints and therapeutic techniques. He saw this problem clearly and solved it by building his ideas and treatment methods on *observable interpersonal relationships*. These consist of the verbal and nonverbal things that go on between people, and they can be seen, heard and felt. They can be observed directly and they can be studied by means of technological equipment such as audiovisual recordings, devices for measuring body responses to interpersonal events, and other kinds of instruments. In their present stage of development, psychology, psychiatry and psychotherapy are not scientific disciplines since most of their principles still are waiting for objective experimental verification; Sullivan's approach holds out the hope that in time these fields can become truly scientific.

This explains the importance of Sullivan's concepts of awareness and unawareness. As noted above, a thought or feeling may be aware or unaware in the same sense that it may be strong or weak and important or trivial. Awareness and unawareness are merely shifting qualities of thoughts and feelings; they have nothing to do with a hypothetical entity called the "mind."

Moreover, the degree of awareness or unawareness of a thought or feeling can be objectively demonstrated by talking with a patient about it. An observer can determine the extent to which the patient knows of its existence, and he can measure some of the patient's body reactions as he comes to grips with it. Additional data can be obtained by observing the patient's interactions with people and with the observer himself. These things, and many kindred ones, move the subject of awareness and unawareness into the sphere of scientific study and out of the realm of unprovable speculation.

The purpose of psychotherapy is to help the patient become aware of his interpersonal relationships and their concomitant feelings and thoughts. This is done by exploring these relationships in alert dialogues and, in some cases, by direct observation of interpersonal relationships.

As we shall later discuss in various contexts, *Sullivan feels that a person has emotional health to the extent that he is aware of his interpersonal functioning.*

AWARENESS AND UNAWARENESS IN PSYCHOTHERAPY

One of the therapist's main tasks is to note places where the patient seems unaware of the significance of things that have occurred in his relationships with people. By his questions and comments he helps the patient to acquire awareness about them.

Patient: While I was trying to decide where I would do my postgraduate work, my father found me a good part-time job at the place where he worked. This more or less settled whether I'd leave home and attend Berkeley or stay at home and go to M.U.

Therapist: Was the money you made on this job important?

Patient: No, but it was useful, and my father had gone to a lot of trouble to get it for me.

Therapist: Did you live at home the entire time you worked on your Ph.D.?

Patient: Yes, there seemed to be no reason for moving out of my parents' home; it would have been much more expensive.

Therapist: Do you think your father found this continued dependence on him and your mother gratifying?

Patient: I think he probably did.

Therapist: Do you think this is worth looking into?

In this condensed dialogue the therapist is helping the patient to become *aware* of how his parents' overprotectiveness has molded him into a socially insecure person.

In other instances the therapist tries to increase the patient's awareness of his characteristic ways of dealing with people in his day-to-day life, and he helps him to see how these patterns are the products of former interpersonal relationships.

The same patient and therapist cited above are talking in a later session.

Patient: After I got my Ph.D., I was offered a transfer to the personnel department of the company, with a much higher salary, and I accepted. I went on living at home; my father and I rode to work in the same car pool.

Therapist: Did you consider moving out of your parents' home at this time?

Patient: A couple of friends wanted me to join them in renting an apartment in Crestwood. I thought about it, but decided not to.

Therapist: How did you feel about moving out of your parents' home?

Patient: I guess it made me a little tense. I'd never lived away from home before.

Therapist: What do you mean by "tense"?

Patient: It scared me a little. I'd never lived with strangers before.

Therapist: Strangers? Was that your word or someone else's?

Patient: My mother and father called them that. I knew one of them pretty well, and the other one seemed all right. Still, I was uneasy about the idea of leaving home.

Therapist: Do you think this was because your parents had always made it so easy for you to live at home, and looked on people outside the home as "strangers"?

Much material, which usually would take far longer to explore in actual therapy, is abbreviated in these few lines; however, they demonstrate how the therapist helps the patient to become more aware of his feelings and to understand how long-term interpersonal relationships have caused him to be the kind of person he is.

In other instances the therapist helps the patient to become more aware of the meaning of his acts.

Patient: I told him that if we couldn't agree on it there was no reason to go on seeing each other.

Therapist: And did your decision lead to breaking up with him?

Patient: Yes, it wasn't a big point, but I felt strongly about it.

Therapist: Do you think it was important enough to justify breaking up?

Patient: I thought so at the time.

Therapist: Do you think so now?

Patient: I guess not. It was like my other relationships with men that we've talked about. I used a little thing to end a relationship that I was getting uncomfortable about.

Therapist: What do you mean by "uncomfortable"?

The therapist is here helping the patient to become aware that an argument with her boy friend had more significance than a casual difference of opinion.

Psychotherapy is possible because the therapist can see more in a patient's words and acts than the patient can. The patient communicates more than he knows. The therapist also is less hampered by inhibitions, and he has acquired expertise in investigating interpersonal relationships. He knows more than the patient about the things that are probable in relationships between people, and he is more skillful in forming hypotheses that can be tested in subsequent explorations.

Awareness is a complex process involving both intellectual and emotional assimilation of previously unperceived things. It is more complicated than merely "finding out." As a rule, it requires approaching an issue many times from different points of view, and examining it in the contexts of various kinds of interpersonal associations.

The final consolidation of awareness after much therapeutic work usually necessitates its clear formulation in words. Sullivan emphasizes that *a person is aware of his interpersonal experiences and emotional functioning to the extent that he can formulate them in words; in some cases such formulation may involve no more than articulate awareness within himself; however, awareness is much sounder if it is communicated to another person.* Sullivan feels that many things that are said to be repressed are merely unperceived, unformulated and uncommunicated.

HELPING THE PATIENT TO MAKE SENSE OF HIS LIFE

One of the therapist's major tasks is to help the patient comprehend how his past experiences and current situations make him the kind of person he is and cause him to do the things he does. The patient in time sees that acts and attitudes which seem haphazard or frankly irrational are produced by what has happened to him throughout his life. In simple terms, as some clinicians have expressed it, the therapist helps the patient to write his own life history and to make sense out of it.

In carrying out this task, the therapist in many instances defines a problem; he and the patient then work on it until it leads into still another problem, which they define and explore. The therapist, for example, may say, "Minor failures and shortcomings make you feel inadequate and worthless. Perhaps we can examine this. Can you think of a recent incident in which this has happened?" In another case the therapist may say, "Aggressive people frighten you. Maybe we should take a closer look at this. Let's begin with your relationship with Norman, since this seems a case in point. . . ."

In this kind of work Sullivan pays much attention to *details*; even minor ones may be quite revealing.

Therapist: Where were you standing when he said that?

Patient: I was at my desk. I had gone to it when he came in.

Therapist: And where was he?

Patient: He was standing in the center of the room with a lot of papers in his hand. He kept rattling them as he talked.

Therapist: Was the desk between the two of you, or at one side?

Patient: It was between us. He seemed annoyed about all the papers and cardboard filing boxes I had stacked on it; he said they gave the office a messy appearance.

Therapist: When you have these arguments with him, is there usually a desk between the two of you?

Patient: Well, yes. I guess I more or less retreat behind it when I see him coming. You can tell by the way he walks in the door whether he's mad about something.

Therapist: Do you feel more comfortable with a large piece of furniture between you and him at these times? Does it seem to protect you?

Patient: Maybe. You can never tell what he's going to do or say.

Therapist: What would your feelings be if there were no desk between the two of you when these quarrels occur?

At first glance attention to this detail about a desk may seem picayune; however, such things often disclose a good deal. To a certain extent therapy consists of the careful examination of innumerable details. The crucial point is, of course, that attention is concentrated on the *meaningful* details. The therapist, by noting the patient's verbal and non-verbal reactions in response to the interpersonal event being discussed, directs attention to the important details. He does not allow therapy to become mired in inconsequential ones.

The preceding dialogue continues.

Patient: I guess I'd feel pretty uncomfortable if there were nothing between him and me when he's angry. I'd feel, well, sort of exposed and defenseless.

Therapist: Why?

Patient: I'm not sure. Sometimes I think he'd hit me, or shove me around. I really don't know what I'm afraid of.

Therapist: In the 12 years you've worked in that office, has he ever done that to you, or to anyone else?

Patient: No, he rants a lot, but he's never put a hand on anybody.

Therapist: Then why are you so afraid of his hitting you? Can you connect this fear with any other similar situation in your life?

Patient: I guess it's the same way I felt when I was a kid during my mother's temper tantrums.

Therapist: Can you tell me about those temper tantrums, and how you felt during them?

Attention here to a seemingly insignificant detail has opened the way to discussing another problem; it perhaps is the initial step in relating current emotional difficulties to old interpersonal traumas.

An experienced, alert therapist knows the things that often are important in interpersonal incidents, and he directs therapeutic attention to them. He also is attentive to significant details which are missing in the patient's account of an event or relationship. The therapist frequently gets his clues from nonverbal aspects of the patient's behavior; vocal intonations, facial expressions, body postures and similar things draw attention to meaningful areas.

For example, returning to the dialogues immediately above, the therapist may notice that at tense moments the patient often increases the distance between himself and the therapist, or puts some physical barrier between them. Thus, the patient may at anxious times lean back stiffly in his chair and cross his arms upon his chest; he may at other times cross one leg over the other and clasp his hands upon it, thus putting a barrier of legs, hands and arms between himself and the therapist. This may lead the therapist to wonder if the patient customarily tries to put things between himself and others when he is tense. Good psychotherapy requires continuous, alert observation; an inattentive therapist is an ineffective one.

The therapist is particularly observant of *changes* in the patient's typical ways of dealing with people. For example, he may ask, "Isn't this different from the way in which you usually handle problems of this kind? Looking back on what you generally have done in situations like this, did you act differently this time?" Having established that a change had occurred, the therapist and the patient begin to examine why it did. The therapist's attention also is aroused by unexpected attitudes and acts, and by the absence of customary patterns in the patient's account of his current and past relationships.

In inquiring about things that have been left out of descriptions of interpersonal events, the therapist, for instance, may say, "Do you think it's significant that you didn't mention that she was in the room when this happened? Did you think of that while you were telling me about it and decide to leave it out, or did you forget about it? Did her presence change the situation in any way?" Such questions are, of course, separated by stretches of dialogue between the patient and the therapist.

A therapist sometimes employs an *induced conclusion* in helping a patient's actions and feelings make sense to him. "Well, I think we can now see why you react in this manner in this kind of situation. Because of these experiences early in your life you sense in each relationship of this type a threat to. . . ." "Your reactions are not meaningless, or pointless or even weird, as you fear; they make sense in terms of all the things we have been considering. . . ."

Usually, however, an *induced conclusion* has more impact if put in the form of a question: "Well, is it so remarkable that under these circumstances you always tend to feel inadequate and to withdraw from people?" Sullivan often did this with a touch of melodrama: "And as a result of all this a person feels he is worthless and inadequate? How in the world do we come to such a conclusion?"

THE TACTICS AND STRATEGY OF THERAPY

Psychotherapy proceeds in three general steps, or stages.

(1) The patient and the therapist examine and clarify interpersonal events in the patient's life. Sullivan refers to this as "the establishment of facts."

(2) On the basis of established facts and well explored events, general formulations are constructed about the patient's interpersonal relationships and emotional functioning.

(3) The validity of these general formulations is tested by further examination of the patient's experiences from various points of view and in diverse kinds of interpersonal relationships.

This process, of course, does not go on as mechanically as these numbered steps might suggest. In actual psychotherapeutic practice one stage merges imperceptibly into another. There also is much overlapping; on some occasions two or even three phases may be going on at the same time. However, this general framework is always in the background to orient the therapist.

To present an example of this process as it actually occurs in therapy would require a great deal of space. However, in a very condensed, simplified manner it is demonstrated in the following three dialogues. Each of the three stages is indicated in italics before the dialogue which illustrates it.

1. *The establishment of facts about what goes on in the patient's life.*

Patient: I stayed at the office until 8:30 and finally finished the report. I turned it in to Mrs. Crawford first thing the next morning. She told me to leave it on her desk, and she went on with what she was doing.

Therapist: And how did you feel?

Patient: I was worried and tense. I waited all day to see what she'd say about it; she'd strongly criticized it the first time. However, she didn't say anything, and I guessed it was all right.

Therapist: Is this the way Mrs. Crawford usually handles your reports?

Patient: She's almost never happy with them the first time I write them. I try to do them the way she wants, but I don't seem to get them right. Even when she accepts them, she usually has a lot of complaints.

Therapist: Do you think that perhaps by constant criticism and withholding praise Mrs. Crawford keeps you on a treadmill and gets a lot of work out of you?

In this abbreviated interchange an interpersonal event in the patient's life has been examined. The therapist's final question opens a new area for exploration about this type of event.

2. *On the basis of established facts a general formulation is made about an aspect of the patient's interpersonal life.*

Patient: I guess that after my first two years of college my father was satisfied with how I was doing; anyway, he didn't hassle me anymore. During the first two years he had constantly complained that I wasn't working hard enough, that I could do a lot better, and that he was spending a lot of money on my education and I was just playing around.

Therapist: It seems from what you say about what goes on in your life—at work, between you and some of your friends, between you and your parents and in other situations—that some people control you by criticizing you and withholding praise and affection. They make you feel inadequate and thus get submissiveness, or more work or other things out of you. They do this regardless of how competent and hard working you are.

In these few sentences the therapist has put forward a hypothesis about a significant feature of the patient's relationships with people.

3. *The validity of the general formulation (hypothesis)
   is tested by examining other interpersonal relationships
   in the patient's life.*

Therapist: And how did your husband react to that?

Patient: He didn't like it. He said he was under a lot of
pressure at the office and I'd have to do more to make a
good impression on his boss and his boss's wife. So,
I'm joining that group his boss's wife is organizing; I'm
signing up for a lot of work in it. I really don't have the
time and I don't like the work, but if Harold feels I
should do it I will.

Therapist: And has your husband commented about your
doing all these things?

Patient: No, he hasn't said much. He's pretty much tied up
with problems at the office, I guess.

Therapist: Does it seem like this is the old pattern again? Is
your husband controlling you by a combination of hand-
ing out criticism and withholding praise?

The therapist and the patient are here testing the validity
of the hypothesis set up in stage 2 by examining another of
the patient's relationships.

After a large number of interpersonal incidents have been
examined in various areas of the patient's life, this hypothesis
will, or will not, be validated. This process gradually enables
the patient to develop new insights and to assimilate them
emotionally; it will permit her to evolve healthier ways of
handling her relationships with people.

This insight and its validation open the way for examining
further features of the patient's emotional and interpersonal
functioning. Why is she so sensitive about incidents that
threaten her self-esteem? Why does she feel inadequate when
people manipulate her in this way? Why hasn't she been able

to see this repetitive interpersonal pattern until it is revealed in psychotherapy? What are the anxieties that lock her into this unrewarding, painful way of interacting with others? Psychotherapy progresses by going in this manner from one area and insight to the next.

The formulation of hypotheses and the confirmation of them by the process Sullivan terms *consensual validation* will be covered in much more detail in Chapter 6. The fundamental principles of this aspect of psychotherapy have been sketched here to indicate some of the broader goals of the development of awareness in psychotherapy.

THE BASIC THERAPEUTIC PROCESS: A SUMMARY

Sullivan feels that no one has marked difficulties in living if he has a good understanding of what is occurring between him and other people; such understanding embraces awareness of the impacts of other people on the individual and the effects of his feelings and actions on them.

The therapist's task is to explore with the patient the threats and meanings that various kinds of interpersonal relationships in his life have for him. This often requires that the origins of his interpersonal patterns be traced to their formation in his childhood and early adolescence. Present anguish must be understood in terms of its sources and history.

In the strict sense of the word, the therapist is never called upon to "cure" anyone. His job is to help the patient remove the turmoil which prevents him from achieving satisfying interpersonal relationships. When these blocks have been removed, the patient spontaneously moves forward into healthy relationships with people in a wide spectrum of living.

The patient gradually sees that much more emotional comfort can be obtained by abandoning sick interpersonal patterns than by continuing in them. This achievement helps him to examine other painful situations in his life and to develop more effective ways of dealing with them.

People try to live with as little anguish as possible and to get as much satisfaction from life as they can. This pressure pushes them forward in seeking solutions for their difficulties.

As noted above, Sullivan often states as a basic principle that *a person achieves mental health to the extent that he becomes aware of his interpersonal relationships* and he often replies with these words when patients ask, "What is wrong with me?" "What can I do to get well?" and "What is the treatment accomplishing?" The term *aware* in this context includes a wide variety of emotional and ideational factors; it embraces many things the person *feels* and *thinks*.

Once the patient's anxiety and interpersonal blocks begin to decrease because of treatment, much spontaneous progress occurs in the hours outside the therapeutic sessions. The patient solves many emotional and interpersonal difficulties which his emotional turmoil formerly prevented him from working out. Improvement also continues after treatment ends; emotional health acquires a forward momentum that continually aids the patient in confronting and solving his problems in living.

Chapter 3

The Handling of Anxiety and the Flow of Communication

Sullivan uses the word anxiety in a special way. *He employs it to designate all forms of emotional anguish. Anxiety thus includes apprehensiveness, tenseness, fearfulness, guilt, feelings of inadequacy, feelings of personal worthlessness, shame, self-loathing, eerie feelings of personality change, and all other forms of emotional distress.* Anxiety varies in degree from scarcely noticeable apprehensiveness to incapacitating panic.

Sullivan feels that dividing emotional distress into categories such as anxiety, guilt, feelings of inadequacy, and others is artificial and clinically invalid. It is sounder to use the term anxiety in a comprehensive sense, while recognizing that it has various degrees and aspects.

This broad use of the term anxiety may at first seem strange to mental health professional workers who are accustomed to hearing it employed in a much more restricted way. However, if a professional person examines his own feelings during a truly upset period, he or she will as a rule find it difficult to divide and label his emotional turmoil in categories such as anxiety, feelings of inadequacy, guilt and others. In my opinion, careful self-examination during periods of emotional turbulence demonstrates the validity of Sullivan's viewpoint.

THE OBSTRUCTIVE ROLE OF ANXIETY

Strong emotional distress (that is, anxiety) obstructs the patient-therapist dialogue. It causes the patient either to distort the material he is discussing or to digress into trivial subjects.

One of the therapist's continual tasks, therefore, is to keep the patient's anxiety down to a level at which it does not hinder exploration of his interpersonal and emotional difficulties.

This is an important principle in Sullivan's psychotherapy. Various facets of it are made clear in the following illustration. If during an interview a patient suddenly has acute abdominal colic caused by a kidney stone or a gallstone, he is unable to go on discussing his life experiences; his severe pain prevents him from working on the psychotherapeutic task at hand. If a little while later his pain decreases somewhat, he may be able to resume talking about his emotional problems, but his continuing discomfort will cause him to omit important details and to be distracted from seeing the significance of many things he and the therapist are considering. *The pain of acute anxiety operates similarly.* In many instances anxiety hampers an interview more than physical pain would, since the anxiety is produced by what is being discussed and can be alleviated by abandonment of the topic.

Anxiety is precipitated frequently during psychotherapy. As the patient comes to grips with his problems, he feels tension, or guiltiness, or self-loathing or some other form of emotional discomfort. If a patient does not have surges of anxiety from time to time, he probably is not discussing important aspects of his life, because it is his painful interpersonal relationships, past and present, that have caused his difficulties.

The therapist must be continually alert to upswings of anxiety in patients. Anxiety often indicates to the therapist

which areas of the patient's life are troubled and merit investigation, but it also must be kept down to tolerable levels if
effective work is to go on.

This is illustrated in the following abbreviated dialogue.

Patient: When things started to go wrong between Debbie
and me, it seemed like it was the story of my first marriage all over again. Living with a woman seems to bring
out the worst in me. I became cold and bitchy, and
everything, well, uh . . . (wavers and stops talking). . . .

Therapist: Do you feel it's a disaster that you went through
two difficult marriages?

Patient: No, but the same thing seemed to happen in both of
them. I began to pick at her, and when she fought back I
became sullen. I did the same thing with Margaret. Fred
Martin, who works with me, says his problems with his
wife are different; he tries to tie her down too much,
and she resents it . . . (talks about Fred Martin's marital
difficulties for a couple of minutes). . . .

Therapist: Is it easier to talk about Fred Martin's problems
than your own?

Patient: Each of my marriages was a mess. It would have
been better for me, and better for Margaret and Debbie,
if I had never married at all . . . (silence). . . .

Therapist: You've had some painful marital problems, but I
haven't heard anything that sounds insoluble.

The use of pointed questions (which should be expressed
with reassuring vocal inflections), as in the therapist's first two
entries in this dialogue, is characteristic of the way Sullivan
himself sought to reduce anxiety when it started to obstruct an
interview. Other therapists might employ less emphatic techniques. Each therapist slowly forms a repertory of techniques
that work best for him.

In this dialogue the patient, while discussing the failures

of his marriages, begins to express feelings of inadequacy, and rising anxiety causes him to falter and stop talking. The therapist intervenes with an anxiety-reducing question, and the patient begins to talk again. Then the patient's feelings of inadequacy and guilt cause him to digress into talking about the marital problems of a friend. It soon is apparent that this subject is irrelevant to the patient's problems. (In actual psychotherapy, as compared with an abbreviated dialogue like this one, the therapist might let the patient go on at greater length on Fred Martin's marital difficulties to see if there was some similarity to the patient's marital problems.) To discuss this unrelated topic at length would rob the interview of its usefulness; it would also tend to establish an undesirable pattern of allowing the patient to digress for long periods into unprofitable areas each time he began to feel anxious.

The therapist therefore intervenes with a question which (1) points out tactfully to the patient that he has digressed and (2) brings him back to talking about his own marriage. However, his anxiety continues to hinder him, and the therapist makes an anxiety-reducing statement (the final item in the dialogue) that is designed to facilitate further exploration of the patient's marital problems.

There is a subtle paradox about anxiety. Mild or moderate degrees of it motivate a person to seek psychotherapeutic help and to persist in it, but large amounts of it block psychotherapy. If a person has no discomforts and dissatisfactions in his interpersonal life, he is unlikely to come for therapy, or to persist in it if he does come. On the other hand, acute anxiety during therapy causes him to balk, or to talk about irrelevant things, and to get little from the therapeutic experience. Anxiety is thus both the incentive for psychotherapy and its most common obstacle; keeping it within useful limits is one of the therapist's main tasks.

THERAPEUTIC USE OF ANXIETY

Each upsurge of anxiety in psychotherapy provides the therapist with an opportunity to clarify some aspect of the patient's life; at the same time anxiety often must be reduced to allow the interview to go on. This is illustrated in the following dialogue.

Patient: For four weeks I haven't been able to get an erection. I've tried at least two or three times a week, and my wife must be getting fed up with this. If it goes on there won't be much point in continuing our marriage. I'm beginning to dread bedtime. During the last week I've sat in front of the TV set drinking until after midnight; I finally go to bed half drunk or fall asleep in the chair and wake up there the next morning. Getting into bed with Laura, and knowing she probably wants it, makes me feel awful.

Therapist: Do you mean that a person is a total failure in life because he hasn't been able to get an erection for four weeks? If he is successful in his work, and a good father to his children, and gets along well in all other ways with his wife, and is liked and respected by his friends, is he completely worthless because of a *short-term* problem like this?

This rhetorical question is intended (1) to reduce the patient's feelings of inadequacy to a tolerable level and (2) to put his problem in a broader context as the initial step in solving it. The therapist and the patient will probably have to deal with a large number of such upsurges of despair as therapy continues.

In another case, illustrating the same principle, the following interchange occurs.

Patient: After some of her tirades about everything I'd ever done wrong, I wished that one of us was dead, and especially her, I guess. Then, when she died in an automobile accident when I was 15, I felt, well, you know, just ... (stops talking). ...

Therapist: Do you feel your reaction to her tirades was unusual? Don't you think it's probable that your brother, your sister and maybe your father also had the same kind of fleeting thoughts during some of your mother's prolonged rages?

Here again the therapist's words are designed (1) to reduce anxiety and (2) to direct the patient's attention to a new aspect of the subject under discussion, the feelings of his siblings and father about his mother's guilt-throwing harangues.

Sullivan feels that therapeutic techniques that mobilize anxiety (which are advocated by some psychiatric writers) are erroneous. If a good dialogue about the patient's interpersonal life is going on, anxiety will crop up frequently, giving the therapist many opportunities to decrease and utilize it. If therapy does not naturally stimulate anxiety from time to time it probably is not dealing with truly significant areas of the patient's life.

ANXIETY AS A BLOCK TO UNDERSTANDING EXPERIENCE

Anxiety hinders the perception and understanding of experience. An anxious person is not aware of many aspects of what is going on between him and other people; he does not grasp the meanings of many events. This is seen most clearly in an individual in a state of panic; he is so upset that he cannot see accurately what is happening around him and within him.

A person in a lesser state of anxiety does not assimilate subtler aspects of the interpersonal incidents in which he is involved. For example, he may not be aware that a rising measure of anxiety causes him to do things which break up the relationship he is in and thus remove him from it. In another case, a person may be unable to see that he camouflages feelings of inadequacy, or guilt or fear with an outburst of anger toward the individual who is mobilizing these feelings in him. In still other cases anxiety causes a person to become inattentive to the attitudes and actions of others, or distracts his attention from important things occurring around him, or pushes him into activities which antagonize and upset others.

Sullivan has a striking way of expressing this. He states that *an anxious person simply does not experience what is happening to him.* Afterward it is as if the event had not occurred. Since the person does not experience the event, or at least significant aspects of it, he learns nothing from it. It does not become part of the aware, assimilated experience which determines his subsequent feelings and actions. The anxiety-ridden experience thus cannot contribute to healthy personality changes.

A central task of psychotherapy, therefore, is to help the patient integrate his anxiety-ridden experiences into the total fund of assimilated experience on which he can draw in his future interpersonal and emotional functioning. This is done by discussing interpersonal experiences in the life of the patient and, at times, by examining what goes on interpersonally between the patient and the therapist during the therapeutic sessions.

An example of the first of these two therapeutic activities is shown in the following condensed dialogue.

Therapist: Can you tell me how this argument between you and Mark began?

Patient: We were going over the sales figures for the April report. He felt that several large orders, on which I had done most of the work, should be partially credited to him. That's typical of how he tries to take credit for work I do. We went over the figures two or three times, and he kept insisting that his role in these sales should be mentioned, and I finally had enough and blew up at him. I guess I used some pretty strong language. Anyway, we stopped working on the report and put it off until later. Both of us got pretty upset.

Therapist: Is your income influenced by how these reports are made out?

Patient: No, but it probably affects how people think about me in the home office. Since Mark is district supervisor, he gets a fixed salary.

Therapist: In making out these reports, are Mark's sales noted separately from those of the salesmen in his district?

Patient: No, all sales are reported on each salesman's page, but when Mark participates in a sale it is starred and a note to that effect is put at the bottom of the page.

Therapist: Do most of the salesmen's monthly reports have a few such starred items?

Patient: I guess so. Mark is a pretty active supervisor.

Therapist: When someone at the home office sees such a starred sale on one of your reports, what do you think happens?

Patient: I don't know. Maybe they think I wasn't able to close the deal myself and had to call in Mark.

Therapist: In other words, *you fear they will think you are inadequate to handle the work you are supposed to do?*

Patient: Yes, I guess that's about it.

Therapist: Do you feel you're constantly on trial to prove your adequacy to do your job?

Patient: Yes, that bothers me a lot.

Therapist: *Do you think your feelings of inadequacy become acute when Mark wants his role in these sales reported, and that you cover up your feelings of inadequacy by becoming angry?*

In this case the patient's feelings of inadequacy and fearfulness prevented him from seeing his supervisor's activities in a realistic manner. His anxiety blocked him from being aware of various things that were going on in this interpersonal situation. These unperceived things therefore did not become part of his assimilated experience. They hence would not influence his feelings and behavior the next time he was in the same situation or a similar one. Put in other words, they did not become part of the aware experience on which he could draw in his interpersonal actions in the future. As a result he would be prone to repeat the same unhealthy behavior many times in subsequent similar events. The therapist's questions and comments were designed to bring these things into his field of awareness so that they would become part of his aware, useful past experience.

When this experience has been examined by the therapist and the patient from a number of different points of view, and perhaps in the contexts of several similar experiences, the patient's awareness of what occurs will be much increased. He will comprehend that in many areas of his life he struggles with feelings of inadequacy and worthlessness; he will see that when an interpersonal event mobilizes these painful feelings (anxiety) he tends to avoid awareness of what is happening by becoming angry at the person who, often unwittingly, arouses feelings of inadequacy in him. In the incident given above, the patient may in time recognize that his supervisor's request for some recognition of his role in these sales is reasonable, and perhaps even routine, in the company for which they work.

The therapist also helps the patient become aware of how anxiety prevents him from experiencing things that occur during the therapeutic hours themselves.

Patient: It's hard to know what went wrong. Randy and I just drifted apart and broke up after living together for a couple of months, but we're still friends. It got stale. It ended like my other two affairs ended; nothing came of it.

Therapist: How was the sexual side of this relationship?

Patient: So-so. I was studying for my final exams and also had my thesis to complete. I was under a lot of pressure. I had to finish my thesis and get my degree to be able to take the job I was to begin in September. It may be that Randy was just a casualty in the academic rat race I was in.

Therapist: Have you noticed that whenever we touch, even lightly, on the sexual side of your relationships with men you start talking about something else? Is there something uncomfortable in considering this aspect of your life?

The therapist here is bringing into the patient's field of awareness something that is going on in the treatment situation itself. The patient's emotional discomfort (anxiety) about some aspect of her sexual life causes her to skip over the therapist's inquiry; she virtually does not notice it. If at a later time she were asked if the therapist brought up her sexual adjustment during this interview, she probably would not remember his question. However, in this exchange the therapist moves it into the central focus of their discussion. *The therapist is trying to bring this area of her life into the body of her understood, assimilated experience so she may draw on it in later interpersonal relationships.*

Because anxiety-laden things do not become part of a patient's assimilated experience, the therapist is frequently faced with the problem of missing data. There are gaps and incongruities in the patient's accounts of his experience. Because of these gaps his experiences often do not make sense; they do not form a coherent pattern. The therapist often must think, and occasionally say, "But this account is not complete. It is inadequate." He and the patient must then explore to find the missing feelings, thoughts, facts and activities that anxiety has prevented the patient from incorporating into his fund of remembered, absorbed experience.

Anxiety often produces hiatuses and distortions in the time sequences of patient's accounts of events and interpersonal relationships. The therapist thus may reflect, "This cannot be so. This must have happened much later than the patient feels it did." He frequently must join the patient in an effort to find out how one thing led to another and to discover how the patient's anxieties have caused him to distort the connections and sequences of events. Checking the opinions and comments of other involved persons, by asking what they said to the patient, may lead to correcting time sequences and establishing accurate connections. For example, the therapist may inquire, "What are the feelings of your wife about the connections of these events?" "Did your mother always stress that this happened after you ran away from home?" In some instances patients could not see things in the past which at the time were obvious to others.

DIVERSE WAYS OF HANDLING ANXIETY

A therapist cannot reduce anxiety until he knows what the patient is anxious about. Sullivan feels that reassurances such as "You're quite upset now, but your distress will be less in a little while" and "Anxiousness like this is common" are not good ways to deal with anxiety. The therapist's questions and statements about anxiety *should specify its nature and point out the general context in which it arises.* For example, the therapist may say, "Do hostile thoughts about your parents always make you feel guilty?" and "People who are facing dissolution of their marriages often feel isolated, frightened and desolate." In each of these instances the therapist indicates the nature of the patient's emotional distress and connects it with the interpersonal situation that is causing it.

If a therapist does not know enough about the nature and interpersonal background of a patient's anxiety he should get more information before attempting to handle it. There are, however, a few exceptions to this rule. The most common one involves people who are on the edge of panic. It may be difficult, or even impossible, to get more information from a panicky person, and the therapist may have to employ non-specific anxiety-decreasing comments; sometimes they must be emphatic and profuse. Resistant, frightened adolescents also may be unable to say much to orient the therapist about the nature and precipitants of upsurges of acute anxiety. It often is better to withdraw from a panic-producing area than to probe it further. "We can let that go for the time being. Returning to your relationship with. . . ." In most cases, however, the patient's anxiety is of a lesser degree and the therapist can use a number of well framed questions to get the information he needs to deal effectively with it.

If a therapist can trace the steps by which a patient has become anxious during an interview, he often can see what the patient is anticipating in the next stage of it. The therapist should at all times have a bird's-eye view of where he and the patient are in an interview. This enables him to glance backward to review the material he and the patient have been discussing and to discern the general direction in which they are proceeding.

The following example illustrates this. As a patient becomes increasingly anxious, the therapist casts his attention backward and notes that for the past half hour they have been discussing the patient's growing interpersonal closeness to a lover; the therapist hence wonders if the patient's increasing anxiety indicates discomfort about what that closeness entails. Does the patient dread that such closeness may lead to domination of him by the other person? Does this closeness stir painful memories of his parents' strife-ridden marriage? Does he fear incompetence as a sexual partner in a long-term relationship? The therapist keeps all options open as he and the patient explore many possible threats that this situation has for the patient.

The therapist may know enough about this patient to have fairly sound ideas about why a close sexual relationship mobilizes anxiety in him. When this is so, he can place the patient's emotional discomfort in its general interpersonal context. For example, he may say, "Your growing uneasiness as you get close to Bill is caused, at least in part, by a terror that in any marriage of your own you will have the misery that characterized the marriage in which you spent your childhood and adolescence, that of your parents."

At times the therapist can diminish anxiety by relating it to its historical setting. "Isn't this feeling of desolate loneliness much the same thing you felt when you many times encountered coldness and anger in your parents?" "Is the irritability you now feel toward me the same thing you have often felt toward teachers, job superiors and others who were, or seemed to be, authoritative persons in your life?" Putting emotional anguish in its historical context helps it to make sense, and it also takes away much of its impact.

In some cases the therapist must deal with the person's

anxiety about being a patient. This as a rule occurs only in the early stages of therapy, and it is less common today than it was in preceding decades. Nevertheless, in some segments of society there is still a strong feeling that a person "ought to be able to manage his own affairs and stand on his own two feet" and "ought not to depend on others to straighten out his problems for him." Therapists still see patients in whom there is an instilled feeling that a truly competent individual ought to be able to "control his mind" and that inability to do so indicates a lack of willpower or poor moral determination. In such cases the therapist may ask, "How do you feel about coming to see me?" "Are you troubled by the feeling that a truly adequate person ought to be able to handle his problems by himself?" "Do any of the people around you reflect this point of view?" When the patient is troubled by such attitudes, the therapist may say, "The only difference between you and a lot of people around you is that you have the honesty and courage to recognize your problems and seek help for them, and they don't" or "People who loudly criticize therapy often are trying to deny that they themselves have problems and could perhaps benefit from it."

A therapist rarely should back away from something a patient wants to discuss, for such reluctance may make the patient feel that the subject is so shameful, loathsome or dangerous that it must not be examined. Even when the therapist feels that a subject is probably irrelevant, trivial or potentially panic-producing, he should let the patient talk about it enough to evaluate it and set it in its proper perspective. Also, the therapist should never give the impression that he himself cannot tolerate discussing some aspect of the patient's life because it is too disgusting or upsetting. In many cases the therapist can define these things. "You seem to have some pressure to talk about this. Well, let's take a look at it and see what's there." "Do you feel I might be so revolted by talking about this aspect of your life that it's unwise to consider it?" "Do you sometimes fear that when I discover how inadequate and worthless you think you are I'll throw up my hands and say, 'There's no point going on with this person'?" In some instances, to quell the patient's anxiousness, the therapist may add, "These are your *fears;* now let's find out the *facts.*"

However, as noted previously, there are occasions when continued examination of a panic-ridden topic would be unwise or even dangerous. Extensive investigation might precipitate a panic or make therapy so painful that the patient would abandon it. In such instances the therapist can make a comment indicating that he understands the situation, and can then direct therapy into another area. "That must have been frightening to go through, but must we talk about it now? Perhaps it would be better to look at your relationship with...."

In most cases Sullivan is skeptical of the value of exploring a patient's fantasies, especially if they have fearful or bizarre tinges. He feels it is more useful to examine what has gone on, and is going on, in the patient's interpersonal life than to investigate introspective daydreams that are largely divorced from interpersonal relationships. However, it at times may be useful to inquire into fantasies *that are closely related to past or ongoing interpersonal activities.* "What kinds of speculations or daydreams did you have about your relationship with him?" "What sorts of daydreams did you have about your future with her?"

Sullivan feels that prolonged, elaborate examination of fantasies as a major method of treatment tends to produce a subtle schism from reality in some patients; this is particularly likely to happen if weird, unrealistic things are encountered in the fantasies. It also trains some patients to engage in long stretches of unguided introspection outside the therapeutic hours, which can be perplexing and frightening. If therapy drifts into this kind of activity, the therapist may say, "Well, daydreaming occupies a fair amount of time in everyone's life; however, we can solve your problems better by studying what goes on between you and other people."

Chapter 4

Security Operations and the Self-System

Sullivan uses the term *security* to designate a state of comfortable, tensionless ease; it is the opposite of anxiety. Security is associated with a sense of personal adequacy and strong self-esteem. An individual who feels secure is free of feelings of apprehensiveness, guilt, worthlessness, and all other forms of emotional distress. Each person is constantly seeking to arrange his interpersonal life in patterns that will give him the largest possible amount of security.

Persistent, complete security is an elusive goal. The constantly changing demands of interpersonal living frequently mobilize a certain amount of anxiety in everyone. Anxiety and security are thus in a continual state of flux. They may be viewed as being on the opposite ends of a seesaw that is rarely motionless.

THE ROLE OF SECURITY OPERATIONS IN EVERYDAY LIFE

In his constant efforts to achieve security and diminish anxiety, each person uses interpersonal devices which Sullivan terms *security operations.*

57

A security operation is an interpersonal action by which a person decreases anxiety and increases security. In many instances a security operation is outside the individual's field of awareness; he is not aware of the interpersonal acts and attitudes he employs to quell anguish and achieve emotional comfort.

A security operation may be healthy or unhealthy. In a *healthy* security operation an individual abolishes anxiety and obtains security without impairing his interpersonal and emotional adjustment. A healthy security operation usually increases a person's social effectiveness and emotional stability.

In contrast, an *unhealthy* security operation diminishes anxiety at some cost to the person. It may produce a subtle distortion in his interpersonal relationships or it may precipitate some kind of emotional distress. However, the discomfort he feels as a result of his security operation is less than he would have felt if he had not used it. The diverse kinds of unhealthy security operations produce many of the interpersonal maladjustments, emotional disturbances and personality warps for which people seek psychiatric help.

Every security operation involves *observable interpersonal acts;* in it something occurs between two or more people. Security operations are thus markedly different from Freudian mechanisms of defense and similar processes in other psychiatric systems. Since mechanisms of defense occur in a hypothetical structure termed the mind and are not objectively observable, they cannot be subjected to scientific verification. Sullivan's concept of security operations is consistent with his principle that all processes in psychiatry and psychology must be conceived in ways that permit them to be proved or disproved by directly observable events which any well trained person can evaluate.

A few examples of security operations will be presented to make their nature clear.

Healthy Security Operations

Less attention has been given to healthy security operations than to unhealthy ones. Healthy security operations function smoothly and do not attract the notice of mental health professional workers as much as unhealthy ones do. Hence, less is known about healthy security operations than sick ones.

Sublimation is probably the most common healthy security operation. In it an individual gives acceptable social expression to otherwise unacceptable interpersonal drives. Sullivan's concept of sublimation differs from Freud's concept in a significant way. Sullivan restricts sublimation to acts in which two or more people are involved; by definition, it occurs only when a person does some specific thing in association with another person. For example, sexual drives that would cause social maladjustments if crudely carried out receive delayed, diluted expression in affectionate acts toward friends, other close persons and social groups. Similarly, hostile urges that would create interpersonal chaos if frankly manifested are given outlets in aggressive sports, vocational competitiveness, political rivalries, strong complaints about public issues and many other socially acceptable aggressive acts.

Selective inattention is a security operation that may be either healthy or unhealthy. In selective inattention a person does not perceive various aspects of an interpersonal event in which he is involved; if these facets were observed, they would make the interpersonal relationship less workable. Each individual probably observes only a small percentage of the things occurring in his environment; the rest is peripheral to his awareness, or outside it entirely. The focus of human attention at any particular moment is on a relatively small segment of what is happening.

In selective inattention the individual is *specifically* unobservant of those things which would make an interpersonal relationship unsatisfactory. For example, a woman does not notice selfish or crude acts of her husband which would, if seen, contaminate her affection for him and make her marriage less satisfactory. She *selectively inattends* those things which would impair her happiness. A man similarly is selectively inattentive to many aspects of his wife's interpersonal life which, if scrutinized, would make the marriage less gratifying. It is probable that complete awareness of all aspects of interpersonal relationships would make most of them less satisfying and many of them unworkable. Smoothly operating selective inattention is a universal, continuous security operation that is necessary for successful interpersonal living.

It is obvious, of course, that selective inattention is healthy only up to a certain point. This, however, is true of all healthy security operations; they are healthy only up to the point where they facilitate interpersonal life without obstructing perception of reality to degrees that produce social and emotional maladjustments. The precise point at which selective inattention ceases to be healthy and becomes unhealthy is often a matter of opinion, and varies from person to person and from one epoch in a person's life to another. When selective inattention causes major distortions in an interpersonal relationship it is unhealthy.

It perhaps should be noted in passing that selective inattention is quite different from the Freud's concept of repression. Selective inattention is an *ongoing* interpersonal activity between two or more people. A person can selectively inattend only things that are *going on* in the present. He cannot selectively inattend something that happened in the past. However, things that a person selectively inattends in the present do not become part of his assimilated experience; since he does not perceive them, it is as if they had not occurred. Hence, selectively inattended things do not become part of the fund of experience on which a person can draw in his future attitudes and actions. In contrast, in Freudian repression a great deal of the person's experience is stored in a structure termed the unconscious mind; some of these repressed things are felt to exert continuous or intermittent influence on the individual's behavior, though he is not aware of this.

Selective inattention, like other security operations, can be directly observed and studied by mental health professional workers and social scientists; they can observe two-person and multi-person events in which one or more persons do not perceive things that are occurring. Since selective inattention is observable it can be subjected to scientific scrutiny. Repression, on the other hand, operates entirely in a theoretical body called the unconscious mind; its workings cannot be subjected to direct scrutiny and verifiable experiments. Though it can "explain" much and many things can be said to "corroborate" it, it is conceived in such a way that it is beyond the reach of scientific proof. These features of interpersonal psychiatry and psychology have been noted in earlier ages, but merit attention again in this connection.

Unhealthy Security Operations

Unhealthy security operations quell anxiety at the cost of producing difficulties in the individual's interpersonal relations. We shall at this point do no more than mention unhealthy security operations since they will be discussed at length in the following section on their occurrence in psychotherapy.

THE OCCURRENCE OF SECURITY OPERATIONS IN PSYCHOTHERAPY

A therapist spends much time in psychotherapy dealing with security operations which are distorting the things the patient says and are warping the patient-therapist relationship. When a patient begins to feel apprehensiveness, guilt, personal inadequacy, or some other form of emotional discomfort he is prone to resort to a security operation that diverts the interview from the area which is mobilizing anxiety in him. He does this, of course, in ways of which he is unaware. The security operations he employs are usually the ones he characteristically uses in his day-to-day living with people.

The therapist frequently must detect these security operations and help the patient become aware of them. This is necessary if the interviews are to remain productive. Moreover, by becoming aware of these obstructive security operations, the patient can gradually cease to use them. He thus becomes free of unhealthy security operations which have long been distorting his interpersonal relationships. Also, his ability to be aware of what goes on between him and other people in many kinds of interpersonal situations increases.

Dealing with a security operation involves identification of the emotional distress which sets it in motion. The underlying apprehensiveness, shame, guilt, or other kind of emotional discomfort must be defined, and this should be done in the context of the particular interpersonal setting that mobilized it.

In the following four abbreviated dialogues we shall consider some simple security operations that commonly occur in therapy.

Therapist: Did you begin to feel apprehensive as he spoke?
Patient: He went on explaining things about the house. He pointed out some of its advantages. It's near the freeway and I can get to work easily on it. Also, there are good schools nearby. The value of the property there is bound to go up because of its location. The house is in good

shape. The last owner completely remodeled it, added a family room in the back and . . . (goes on for some time in this vein). . . .

Therapist: Do you think that at times you use this kind of talkativeness about unrelated things to avoid dealing with an issue that makes you feel uncomfortable?

The patient here uses verbosity as a quite simple type of security operation. Confronted with an emotionally painful subject, he flees into a stream of rapid talk on a trivial subject. If the therapist does not intervene, the patient may fill the rest of the interview, and others as well, with such material. Verbosity can paralyze therapy unless it is defined as a security operation. If the therapist allows the patient to employ empty verbosity as a security operation under the assumption that he in time will reveal his problems and work through them, he may spend weeks or months in a kind of treatment that is of little value.

Moreover, this patient probably employs empty talkativeness as a characteristic method for fleeing anxiety in his day-to-day relationships with people. Becoming aware of it and resolving it in the therapeutic situation on numerous occasions enables him to abandon this unhealthy device in other kinds of relationships.

The following brief interchange illustrates another common, simple kind of security operation.

Therapist: Did you feel ill at ease in this situation?
Patient: Yes, that's exactly it. This is just how I felt.
Therapist: Can you describe in more detail how you felt?
Patient: Well, I think you've summed it up pretty well.
Therapist: Complete agreement with me more or less tends to end discussion of this subject, doesn't it?

The patient here shuts off examination of an anxiety-ridden topic by immediate, blanket agreement with the therapist. If this type of security operation is not identified and resolved early in therapy (and many patients employ it much more suavely than in the simplified example given above), therapy soon deteriorates into discussions that have little to do with the patient's problems; material relative to his difficulties is rapidly shoved aside and the focus of attention is shunted onto things that are free of anxiety and of little value to discuss. An inexperienced therapist may go on for weeks or months in such a profitless way, and may even feel that the patient's ready acquiescence indicates "insight." Such therapy may be gratifying to a therapist who does not understand what is going on.

A somewhat less common, simple security operation is outlined in the following short exchange.

Therapist: Did this precipitate feelings of self-doubt in you?
Patient: Of course it did. That's obvious and I've known it for years. I didn't come here to hear things like that. I'd like to find out something new instead of listening to that kind of stuff.
Therapist: Do you think that perhaps you sometimes get angry when confronted with an uncomfortable topic?

In this case the patient uses an angry attack on the therapist as a security operation to deflect attention from a painful subject.

This is a characteristic technique the patient employs in handling anxious situations, and it is occurring in an ongoing relationship with the therapist. Sullivan feels that it has not been "transferred" to the therapist from someone else in the past; he feels that many things which are sometimes called "transference" are merely the characteristic ways patients deal with day-to-day tensions, including those that arise during the therapeutic hours.

The fourth of these simple security operations is sketched below.

Therapist: Did this make you wonder how safe your job was?
Patient: No, I've pulled out of situations like this a lot of times. My work on various deals has drawn a lot of attention, and everybody in the firm knows what I accomplished on the Bancroft project. I'm pretty well known nationally in this field despite the fact that I'm still fairly young. A person of my standing can work his way out of a thing like this without too much trouble.
Therapist: Do you think it's possible that when you feel threatened you try to reassure both yourself and others by impressing people with your importance?

In this abbreviated dialogue the patient attempts to dismiss an anxiety-laden topic by impressing the therapist with his importance. The things he says may be true, but he uses them to deflect examination of an anxiety-laden event in his life. Such self-reassurance may have some value in daily life, but it does not lead to identification of underlying anxieties and learning things from them.

Most security operations are more complex than the relatively simple ones listed above. In a more intricate security operation the patient may develop a persistent inability to understand what is going on in the interview. He misinterprets what the therapist says, distorts the therapist's words to arrive at erroneous conclusions, and is oblivious to the directions of therapy. He is unable to grasp consequences of his actions which are fairly obvious to someone who does not have his anxiety-filled obstacles to comprehending his life.

In other cases the patient may talk glibly about his feelings and relationships with people in a mechanical way, sometimes using scraps of psychiatric jargon, to avoid true involvement in the treatment process; the things the patient talks about are twisted into meaningless non-processes and non-events. He does not come to grips with his emotional anguish and painful interpersonal dealings.

Other security operations are more subtle and more deeply rooted in the individual's personality structure. They consist of general ways in which the patient deals with people in all situations in which anxiety is present or may possibly occur. For example, the ingratiating, deferential behavior of an individual with a passive personality disorder is an elaborate security operation to fend off interpersonal events which might precipitate aggressiveness or annoyance of others toward him. In therapy the passive patient hurriedly agrees with whatever the therapist says, avoids bringing up subjects which he feels might annoy him, and behaves in ways that he feels will please him. Passive patients often are adept in detecting the most minimal signs of puzzlement or displeasure in the therapist, and modify their behavior accordingly. In time they learn to produce material that confirms the therapist's viewpoints about what is wrong with them and how to cure it. Even when the therapist sits out of sight, the patient can detect the impatient rustling of clothing, the bored laying down of a clipboard and a ball-point pen, and the trace of annoyance in the vocal intonations of even the briefest things the therapist says. In addition, of course, the patient scans the therapist's face at the end of every session to see if he appears pleased or bored with what went on.

These things go on outside the patient's field of awareness, of course, and unfortunately they sometimes are outside the therapist's field of awareness. Non-therapy with such a "good patient" may continue for months or years in what amounts to nothing more than *an elaborate, smoothly functioning security operation*. The patient never comes to grips with the emotional distress and personality warps of his life.

In contrast, an individual with an aggressive personality disorder assumes an irritable, bullying stance when anxious areas of his life are approached, and he thus deflects attention, both his own and others', from them. Depending on circumstances, he becomes sullen, or domineering or belligerent. He does this in the treatment situation and in innumerable interpersonal contexts in his daily life. It is his characteristic way of blocking awareness of anxiety-laden events in a comprehensive security operation.

There are many other similar security operations. Much of a therapist's time is spent identifying and dealing with them. They are too complex to be illustrated in sample dialogues; the four dialogues given earlier in this section deal with less embracing and less intricate security operations.

Each person's security operations, both in therapy and in daily life, are characteristic of him. To a large extent they characterize him as the person we know. In defining these security operations in therapy, using both what the patient says about his day-to-day relationships and his interactions with the therapist, the first step is taken in resolving them. By identifying the anxieties that precipitate these security operations and repeatedly studying them as they occur in the patient's family life, vocational activities, social contacts and other areas, the patient gradually achieves a better level of interpersonal and emotional functioning.

THE SELF-SYSTEM

Sullivan employs the term self-system to embrace all the security operations a person customarily employs to defend himself against emotional discomfort (anxiety) in his inter-

personal relationships. The self-system (as noted in other terms in the preceding section) *therefore is characteristic of the individual and to a large extent defines him as the person we know.* When we picture Tom Smith or Nancy Brown to ourselves we are thinking to a large extent of the manifold security operations (comprising the self-system) which each of them uses to protect himself against emotional distress and to live as comfortably as he can.

The concept of the self-system is made clear in the following simplified example. Mark Smith's five main security operations are (1) glib talkativeness, to deflect the attention of both himself and others from anxious topics and events, (2) placating passivity to avoid conflicts with people, (3) flights into solitary pursuits such as reading and work on his stereo equipment when he is in a tense situation or anticipates facing one, (4) preoccupation with small physical dysfunctions such as mild headaches and slight gastrointestinal symptoms to shunt his attention away from interpersonal stresses, and (5) hard work on his job to avoid criticism from his supervisor and friction with his coworkers.

These five security operations give a fair (though by no means complete) picture of the kind of individual Mark Smith is. If a friend of his were to attempt to describe him, he would spend much time talking about Mark's security operations; he would, in essence, be outlining Mark's *self-system.*

The self-system of a person, of course, consists of many more than five security operations. For ease and clarity of presentation, we have merely listed five major ones. If both major and minor ones are included, each person has dozens of security operations; many are healthy and some are unhealthy. Some are employed often and others are infrequently used; some are so small that they are scarcely noticeable and others are so prominent that they are immediately obvious.

Mark of course has other qualities which are not security

operations, and his friend would probably mention some of them in describing him: his good intelligence, musical talent, manual dexterity, and many other things. However, on close scrutiny even these qualities may be intimately linked to his security operations. For example, in his continual efforts to please people and to avoid conflicts, Mark uses his intelligence to a far greater extent than if he were not continually goaded by anxious needs to prove to himself and to others that he is a worthwhile, achieving person. His carefully cultivated musical abilities and manual dexterity likewise make him a useful, valued person in many kinds of social situations. The more one studies Mark, the more diffuse the effects of his self-system are found to be.

It is important to realize that the term *self-system* is a *verbal convenience* which we employ in referring to the sum total of an individual's security operations. *It is not a thing.* Understanding this distinction is essential in comprehending the scientific consistency of Sullivan's system of psychiatry.

The self-system, for example, is not equivalent or in any way similar to the Freudian concept of the *ego*. In Freudian psychiatry the ego is not a verbal convenience; it is an actual entity that is believed to be present in the brain and to operate by an elaborate set of laws. However, the Freudian concept of the ego is postulated in such a way that its existence can never be proved nor disproved; its nature and functions can never be observed and verified in any kind of scientific experiment which all reasonably trained observers can witness. As pointed out in an earlier chapter, the inability of a concept or proposition to be objectively proved or disproved (regardless of how much it "explains") puts the concept or proposition beyond the reach of science.

Sullivan avoids this trap into which so many psychological and psychiatric systems have fallen. He emphasizes that the self-system does not exist in the sense that bushes and trees exist. It is merely a *literary convenience*, a collective term for referring easily to all a person's security operations.

However, *security operations*, as opposed to the *self-system*, are not literary conveniences. *Security operations designate actual interpersonal acts which can be directly observed.* We can see and hear a passive person when he is placating another individual, and we can see and hear an aggressive person when he is bullying someone. These are observable interpersonal events which any well trained person can observe. Security operations thus are subject to scientific study. We can make hypotheses about them and then can test them out by direct scrutiny of what goes on between people.

With these things firmly understood, we can proceed to discuss the role of the self-system in psychotherapy.

The therapist almost constantly is in contact with the patient's self-system. At almost all times some aspect of it is obstructing exploration of the patient's interpersonal life. When anything of importance is being discussed, some degree of anxiety is frequently mobilized; to protect himself against this discomfort, the patient brings some security operation from the self-system's manifold repertory into play. The therapist, in a sense, is continually trying to pierce the patient's self-system and discover the anxious person within.

Herein lies one of the main technical problems, and also one of the major therapeutic opportunities, of psychotherapy. The self-system opposes the work of therapy, but the ways in which it does so constitute many of the problems for which the patient is seeking help. For example, an individual with a passive personality disorder employs deferential, ingratiating submissiveness to obstruct therapy and to deflect it away from considering many of the anxious events of his life; it is this same passivity, and the difficulties it precipitates, that bring the patient to psychotherapy.

Thus, in defining and resolving the patient's security operations (that is, his self-system constituents), the therapist is (1) facilitating the exploration of the patient's life and (2) working to solve his problems at the same time. Such modification of the self-system is one of the major aims of treatment.

MANAGEMENT OF SECURITY OPERATIONS AND THE SELF-SYSTEM IN THERAPY

Most of the preceding pages of this book are, in one way or another, relevant to the therapeutic management of the self-system and its component security operations. Much of the rest of the book will be devoted to giving further details in this work. Each time we have spoken of a technique for handling some kind of emotional anguish (anxiety), we have been talking about a force that can cause a security operation. We shall now consider a few more aspects of dealing with security operations and the self-system.

Sullivan feels that a therapist should not lay bare an anxiety-laden area unless he can offer the patient subsequent anxiety-resolving measures; he should not deprive a patient of a security operation unless he can offer a healthier interpersonal pattern in its place. The therapist should be able to erase, or at least diminish, the mobilized anxiety and reintegrate the patient on a better level of functioning before he and the patient part at the end of a therapeutic session.

To illustrate this principle fully in a sample dialogue would require many pages, with notes on the therapist's vocal intonations and other nonverbal elements of communication; timing and the use of pauses (brief strategic silences) would also have to be indicated. Nevertheless, the preceding paragraph remains of little value to a therapist with a patient in front of him unless a sample dialogue, with all its limitations, is given. The following dialogue deals with passiveness as a security operation, since this security operation can be presented with relative ease and brevity.

Patient: I did as he wanted, and we made up; during the rest of the day we got along fine. It was a good day.

Therapist: Do you usually give in and do what the other person wants in this kind of situation?

Patient: I think it's best to get along with people whenever you can. Like the saying goes, nobody wins a fight; in the end everybody loses. I figure there's enough trouble in the world without my making more.

Therapist: Do you feel there's no other way to settle an issue of this kind than by letting the other person have his way?

Patient: I suppose I could stick up for myself, but it would only lead to a lot of arguments.

Therapist: Let's take a look at that. What do you imagine would have happened if you had held out for what you wanted in this situation with Bob?

Patient: We would have argued all morning, and maybe most of the afternoon. It would have ruined the whole day.

Therapist: Are you sure? Can you tell me about one or two experiences in which persistent assertiveness spoiled an entire day?

Patient: (After a pause) Well, I guess I've never really done it.

Therapist: What do you *fear* might happen if you stuck up persistently for what you wanted? Let your imagination run.

Patient: We would go on and on arguing. Bob would get furious and tell me off. He'd let me have it up one side and down the other. He'd bring up everything I've done wrong in the last five years and throw it in my face. I'd feel awful.

Therapist: What do you mean by "awful"?

Patient: That I'd failed as a wife, and a mother and everything else.

Therapist: Inadequate?

Patient: Yes, a complete failure in everything.

Therapist: Do you think Bob knows that his tirades stampede you by making you feel worthless and inadequate, and as a result he uses them to get his way in everything?

Patient: I don't think so; I'm not sure. It's always been this way between us, even before we were married.

Therapist: Until this point, have you clearly been aware of the fact that Bob dominates you by making you feel inadequate and worthless?

Patient: I suppose I've sensed it, in a way, but I've never said it in so many words, or thought of it in that way.

Therapist: Is it painful to think of your marriage in this way?

Patient: Yes, it makes my marriage look like a dirty game which I always end up losing. And it makes Bob look like he doesn't really care how I feel, or what I want, or what I need, just as long as he gets what he wants. And if that's all I have, why go on with it?

[The therapist and the patient now (1) have identified the patient's passivity as a security operation, (2) have laid bare the kind of anxiety (feelings of inadequacy and worthlessness) which mobilize the security operation, and (3) have given the patient a broader, though more painful, understanding of what goes on in her relationship with her husband.

Much more, however, has occurred. By stripping the patient of her security operation, or at least by laying it painfully exposed, the therapist has made her marriage less tolerable, or perhaps even unworkable. If the therapist cannot furnish the patient with a healthier way of handling this problem, he has, from Sullivan's point of view, committed a technical blunder in psychotherapy.

The therapist proceeds, therefore, in the second phase of this therapeutic process. Again we note that this dialogue is much more condensed than it would be in actual therapy.]

Therapist: Do you think that in dominating you in this way Bob has merely moved into a vacuum created by your passivity? In other words, does he control you in this manner mainly because it works, and would he behave differently if it didn't work?

Patient: I don't know. It's hard to say how it would have been all these years, and would be now, if I hadn't given in to him on everything.

Therapist: Does Bob do with other people, such as his brother, his work associates, his friends and others, the same sort of thing he does with you?

Patient: His brother wouldn't let him get away with it, and so far as I know he doesn't do this at work. Offhand, I can't think of any of his friends he treats in this way.

Therapist: Then what is it in his relationship with you that causes him to treat you in this manner?

Patient: I guess it's me. It throws me off balance, makes me feel inadequate, as you say. And I give in.

Therapist: The question we're working toward is: Is this pattern between you and him something that rises mainly out of his personality, or does it rise out of various things in the relationship between the two of you?

Patient: I've never thought about it in that way, but when you look at it like this I guess it's something that has grown up as much because of me as because of him. If I'd been different, maybe our marriage would be different.

Therapist: What could you do differently?

Patient: Well, I guess I could be firmer on important things.

Therapist: What do you suppose would happen if you were? For example, what do you think would have happened in this incident we've just been discussing?

Patient: He'd really let me have it, like I said. He'd try to make me upset—make me feel inadequate and worthless, to use your words—and I guess I would get upset.

Therapist: Could you stand the pain of that, in an effort to work out a better relationship with him?

Patient: I guess so, if I could see where I was going.

Therapist: What do you think it might lead to?

Patient: To Bob feeling I was impossible to live with, and to us breaking up.

Therapist: Is that what happens when his brother, and the people he works with, and his friends are firm with him?

Patient: No, I guess not. He doesn't break up with them. He thinks the world of his brother, and he likes most of the people he works with.

Therapist: Do you think it's possible that in the long run he might be more considerate of you, think more highly of you, and actually be more affectionate toward you if you were firm with him in reasonable ways?

Patient: I don't know. I guess it's worth a try. Anything would be better than what we have now.

> [The therapist has here suggested a new, healthier interpersonal pattern to substitute for the one he has taken away from the patient. He and the patient have discussed the kind of emotional pain she will feel in putting this new pattern into operation, but they have also examined much evidence which indicates that it

will work and will in time establish her relationship with her husband on a sounder basis. In the future they may discuss how increased assertiveness also may help the patient in other interpersonal relationships.

In clinical practice, of course, an issue of this kind is not solved in a single session. The patient and the therapist must approach it from diverse points of view in the contexts of many interpersonal incidents in the patient's relationship with her husband, and its various emotional facets must be examined, before the new interpersonal and emotional pattern becomes an integral part of her life.]

In some instances it is easier for the therapist and the patient to talk about an anxiety-laden area in terms of *a third party*. When the patient's difficulties are too painful to be discussed in terms of his own experiences, they may be considered as those of a hypothetical other person. This *third party technique* is illustrated in the following brief dialogue.

Therapist: It obviously is very distressing for you to talk about this. Let's shift our focus a bit and talk about the problems of a person whom we shall call Sue Johnson. Sue is a composite of several patients I've seen over the years who faced the same kind of dilemma. Let us say that Sue is 14 and her father has made sexual advances to her. What do you think Sue is feeling?

Patient: I suppose she's scared, and sort of sick inside. She feels like part of her world has just caved in.

By such use of a third party the patient and the therapist can examine a subject that otherwise might be too painful for the patient to talk about. Both of them know that in talking about Sue's panic and revulsion they are really talking about what the patient went through; nevertheless, this technique makes such discussion possible. If at any point this subject becomes too upsetting and threatens to disrupt therapy, the therapist can always drop it. "Well, I think we've talked enough about Sue's problem. There is, of course, more turmoil in her than we've covered, but we can leave that until some other time."

The *third party technique* is often useful in exploring security operations. In the following interchange, continuing with the situation of the previous dialogue, the therapist and the patient define a security operation.

Therapist: I'm puzzled over one thing. How could a girl like Sue Johnson stand the emotional pain of these sexual experiences with her father? What could she do to camouflage the situation and make it tolerable?

Patient: I think she built up a kind of daydream world about it all.

Therapist: What kind of daydream world?

Patient: She daydreamed that her father was not her real father. She imagined that her true father had been divorced from her mother when she was a baby, and the man she now called father was her stepfather and not her true blood father. She even thought that maybe her mother had never actually married this man; they were just living together and pretended to everyone that they were married.

Therapist: Do you mean that Sue acted *as if* he were not really her father, and perhaps even *as if* he were not actually her mother's husband, and that this helped Sue to survive this frightening, guilt-ridden experience?

Patient: Yes, she did something like that. It was all mixed up, but it was more or less like that.

This, incidentally, is an example of what Sullivan calls the *as if* security operation.

There are several variations of the third party technique. For example, the therapist may frame his statements and questions in terms of the things a hypothetical observer of incidents in the patient's life would see. "I wonder what an outsider who was watching this event between you and your mother would have thought. Would he have wondered how really well intentioned she was when she did that?" "If an uninvolved observer had been present, what do you think he would have felt about this?" "If some passerby had been asked to describe what he had seen and heard, what do you think he would have said?"

In another variation of the third party technique, the patient is asked to put himself in the position of another person with whom he has some kind of interpersonal difficulty. "Let's assume for a few minutes that you are Ted. What would you think and feel about your own actions if you had been in Ted's place?" "If you had been Alice, what would you have felt about this incident?" This can be followed by a search for information about the other person's true feelings. "Did Ted say or do anything which indicated that he actually felt that way toward you?" "Did Alice's subsequent behavior suggest that she really thought something like that?" Security operations often are seen in a new light when examined in this way.

If possible, a security operation should first be explored in current, or very recent, interpersonal situations. It can then be examined in events and relationships in the patient's more distant past. For example, the workings of a security operation may first be investigated in the patient's current marital, vocational and social settings, and then in incidents and relationships in his childhood, adolescence and early adulthood. Recent events as a rule can be discussed in more detail and often they have more meaning for the patient since they are concerned with problems about which he still has fresh, vibrant feelings.

Moreover, the patient can use the insights gained in therapy to observe *ongoing* relationships in new ways. He can see his security operations, and those of others, in daily occurrences with close people. His current life thus becomes, in a sense, a laboratory in which he observes new things, tries out new ways of relating to people and notes the reactions of others and himself.

Exploration of events and relationships in the patient's earlier life has, of course, special advantages of its own. The origins of current patterns in early interpersonal situations can be seen, and the long-term consequences of interpersonal relationships and incidents can be examined. Understanding how current interpersonal and emotional patterns have been molded by past experience is a major aspect of helping the patient to make sense of his life and his problems. In most cases both current and past interpersonal living must be explored to give the patient maximum benefit in treatment.

Much of the rest of this book, in both preceding and succeeding pages, discusses ways of resolving unhealthy security operations. Though our main attention in the following chapters will be on other facets of psychotherapy, we shall often be indirectly talking about sick security operations and ways of resolving them.

Chapter 5

The Formulation and Testing of Hypotheses: Consensual Validation

CONSENSUAL VALIDATION

Consensual validation is a central feature of Sullivan's psychotherapy. In it the therapist and the patient achieve a *consensus* about some aspect of the patient's experience, and this consensus is then *validated* by repeated examinations of many incidents in his life.

For example, the patient and the therapist may reach a tentative consensus that the patient by crude, tactless acts breaks up each relationship in his life that threatens to become intimate, and that he does so because painful experiences in childhood and adolescence cause him to fear exploitation by any person with whom he forms a close relationship. This tentative *consensus* is *validated* by examining many aspects of it in the patient's current and past life events and relationships.

In such validation the therapist and the patient keep open minds about other hypotheses which might explain the data equally well and are always ready to examine evidence which might disprove the hypothesis.

The word *consensus* may at first glance convey an incorrect impression, since its general usage has changed much in the decades since Sullivan first employed it. It has become almost a jargon expression employed by journalists to describe agreements among politicians, civic groups and others, or the consolidation of public opinion on an issue. As such, it has the connotation of deliberate, methodical reasoning in prolonged discussion.

This is not what Sullivan means by consensus. To him consensus implies the gradual absorption of new insights; in this process, emotional and intellectual factors are both important. Consensus involves new ways of feeling, of relating to people and of viewing interpersonal life. It is not something coldly agreed upon, but a new manner of experiencing events and relationships with people.

Each new concept, or hypothesis, about the patient's interpersonal living and emotional functioning must be validated by testing it out in examination of the patient's life experiences. This involves evaluation of much experience which supports it and scrutiny of any experience which may be against it. The therapist must ask himself, "Is there any other formulation concerning this part of the patient's life which explains the data equally well? Is there any concept which explains it better?" Only when the concept is fully verified in this manner can it be considered *consensually validated*.

The word *validation* here does not have the mechanical, meticulous connotations that it does in physical sciences such as physics and chemistry. There is no single experiment or group of criteria by which a concept is validated in psychotherapy. Psychotherapeutic validation is a gradual process involving detailed consideration of many experiences from various points of view.

THE FORMATION AND TESTING OF HYPOTHESES

As the work of therapy proceeds, the therapist begins to form hypotheses about what is wrong with the patient. He puts these hypotheses into words and he and the patient begin to examine them. The therapist does not seize on the first concept that comes to mind, nor does he throw hypotheses helter-skelter at the patient. He waits until he has sufficient data gathered from a variety of interpersonal experiences, so that any hypothesis he advances has a good chance of being substantiated by further exploration.

Prematurely proposed hypotheses can damage psychotherapy. The patient may seize upon an inaccurate or irrelevant hypothesis and work on it for hours, weeks or months. It may become a defense against exploring his true interpersonal difficulties. This may be a substitute for the more uncomfortable process of talking about the things that lie at the core of his problems. An inexperienced therapist can spend long periods of time in such unprofitable work. In some unfortunate instances an entire course of treatment may be consumed by such non-processes in pseudopsychotherapy.

Sullivan's term *hypothesis* is perhaps a misleading word in discussing this subject in the last quarter of the twentieth century; it has a cold, mechanical ring. It has never gained widespread acceptance among mental health professional workers. In attempting to find a more acceptable term, I have, since its initial publication in an article I wrote in 1952 (*American Journal of Psychotherapy*, volume VI, page 677, October) used the expression *tentative interpretation* as a substitute for *hypothesis*. I feel it is more acceptable to many mental health professional workers and more accurately conveys to today's professional audience what Sullivan means by *hypothesis*. From this point onward, therefore, the terms *ten-*

tative interpretation and *hypothesis* will be employed as interchangeable synonyms.

The formulation of a hypothesis or tentative interpretation and its subsequent validation are illustrated in the following dialogue. For clarity and ease of presentation the dialogue is quite condensed, but it nevertheless brings out the principles involved.

Therapist: Does it seem that any situation in which you are in competition with other people makes you feel apprehensive and ill at ease? [*In the form of a question, the therapist is putting forward a tentative interpretation, or hypothesis.*]

Patient: I've never thought about it in that way. However, I know I don't like any kind of direct rivalry with other people, and I try to avoid it.

Therapist: Can you tell me about any recent experience in which you found yourself competing with one or more people? [*The therapist is seeking information which validates or invalidates his tentative interpretation.*]

Patient: Well, about four months ago three of us were being considered for sales manager of the downstate district. Everybody knew that one of us would get it. I've known the other two men for a long time, and I didn't like to be in that position. I figured that if I got the job I'd lose one or both of them as friends. They wouldn't say anything, of course, and on the surface everything would go on as usual; however, underneath they'd resent me and things would never be the same again.

Therapist: And what do you think would be the consequences of that?

Patient: Each of them would have a chip on his shoulder against me. They'd be waiting for me to mess up an important deal, or to lose a big contract, or to overbid on a project and get the company into trouble. One false step and they'd be down on me. They could make it tough for me.

Therapist: In other words, you'd fear reprisals.

Patient: I suppose so.

Therapist: Does that happen every time someone gets promoted in your company?

Patient: Well, no. I guess I can't think of any time things like that actually happened. But they *could* happen, and that worried me a lot. When the decision was coming to a head, I didn't sleep well for a couple of weeks, and I had a lot of headaches and stomach trouble. I dreaded going to the office because I'd meet the other two men there almost every day.

Therapist: [He and the patient discuss other interpersonal incidents similar to this one. Having explored evidence which supports this tentative interpretation, the therapist goes on to seek evidence which might disprove it]. Can you think of any kinds of competition with other people in which you *are* comfortable?

Patient: Well, when I'm in a group that's competing with some other group I feel all right. I'm on the company basketball team and at our church I'm on a fund-raising team that's pitted against other teams to see which one can raise the most money for a new building. Those situations don't bother me; in fact I more or less enjoy them.

Therapist: In those situations you are not *individually* competing with other persons. Do you think that is what makes the difference?

Patient: Maybe so. When I used to play golf, I always worried about how the other players would feel if I won. I suppose that's why I gave up playing it.

Therapist: Putting all this together, it seems that competing with other people on a one-to-one basis makes you feel apprehensive; it upsets you a good deal. However, when you're in a group that's competing with other groups you feel comfortable, and even enjoy it somewhat. [*The therapist is here altering his original tentative interpretation (hypothesis) since further data on the patient's interpersonal experience have only partially validated it and require this modification.*]

There is, of course, much more to explore in this aspect of the patient's life; this aspect, in turn, is only a small facet of a much larger personality feature. From one to several or more interviews may be spent examining this subject in a number of diverse interpersonal settings. In the course of this exploration, the tentative interpretation probably will be further modified until the patient and the therapist have definitely clarified this aspect of the patient's interpersonal life. *The patient and the therapist will then have reached full consensual validation about it.*

When he advances a hypothesis the therapist should be careful to mobilize as little anxiety as possible in the patient. He makes his tentative interpretation in a way that does not assault the patient's self-esteem and feelings of personal adequacy. The interpretation should be sufficiently anxiety-free to invite inquiry; it should not deter examination of the topic at hand by making it painful and upsetting.

This principle is illustrated in the following two examples which contrast incorrect (upsetting) and correct (anxiety-free) ways of making a tentative interpretation.

Therapist: [*He here mobilizes strong feelings of personal inadequacy in the patient, making further exploration of this area difficult or impossible*]. Do you think that your angry outbursts constitute one of the main reasons why you find yourself completely isolated in your vocational and social situations?

Therapist: [*Advancing the same hypothesis in a way that does not arouse feelings of inadequacy*]. Put yourself for a moment in the place of someone toward whom, perhaps justifiably, you became angry. Do you feel he might tend to avoid you afterward?

It would be an error to dismiss the difference between these two ways of making a tentative interpretation as little more than a matter of terminology or cleverness with words. The difference often determines whether the therapist will be able to help the patient solve his problems in this area.

The following two examples provide another illustration of this principle.

Therapist: [*Mobilizing panic and shutting off a topic*]. Do you feel it's possible that your alternating feelings of closeness and revulsion toward your sister during adolescence were related to fluctuating sexual attraction between the two of you?

Therapist: [*Putting forward the same hypothesis in a way that perhaps stirs up some anxiousness but does not arouse panic, and thus permits further examination of the subject*]. Do you feel that at times during your adolescence your relationship with your sister stirred up feelings that frightened you in any way?

Incorrect and correct ways of advancing a hypothesis are further illustrated in the following two examples.

Therapist: [*Arousing feelings of self-loathing in the patient by the manner in which he makes a tentative interpreta-*

tion]. Do you feel that people easily perceive your paralyzing insecurity and indecisiveness, and hence exploit you since they know you are powerless to prevent them from doing so?

Therapist: [*Presenting the same hypothesis in a way that does not cause self-loathing*]. Do you feel that people, perhaps almost without knowing it, tend to be bossy toward you because of your trouble in making firm decisions?

The therapist is particularly careful in presenting hypotheses to schizoid, or frankly schizophrenic, patients; he often waits until he feels there is a high degree of probable validity in his interpretations. An incorrect tentative interpretation makes a schizoid person feel that the therapist has little understanding of his problems; he has experienced much insensitivity to his needs and feelings in most of his close relationships, and any evidence of similar insensitivity in the therapeutic relationship is likely to dampen it badly. Hence, to such a patient the therapist frequently presents a hypothesis piecemeal, testing out its validity in fragments.

For example, with a schizoid or schizophrenic patient the therapist does *not* say, "It seems that closeness to people frightens you and makes you fear exploitation by them; these feelings cause you to retreat from them." Instead, he breaks this into three separate interpretations, testing each one out in different explorations, and perhaps in different interviews. Thus, this hypothesis is divided into (1) "It seems that closeness to people upsets you in some way." After exploring and consensually validating this, (2) the therapist asks, "Do you fear that after establishing closeness with people they will exploit you, and that you will be powerless to do anything about it?" Finally, the therapist completes the presentation of his tentative interpretation, or hypothesis, by (3) asking, "Do you think that perhaps you withdraw from close contacts with people rather than expose yourself to this feared exploitation?"

The therapist does not expect, and often does not want, blanket agreement by the patient to a hypothesis he advances. *He wants his hypothesis to serve as a basis for exploring its validity in many interpersonal settings in the patient's life.* After it is consensually validated, the tentative interpretation opens the way to broaching still further hypotheses, which in turn must be explored; this process leads to a continually broadening investigation of the patient's life.

SPECIAL TECHNIQUES IN THE VALIDATION
OF HYPOTHESES

At times it is useful in psychotherapy to point out that there often are two sides, if not more, to every story, and that the patient and the therapist may be considering only one of them. In examining this possibility the therapist may say, "Perhaps we should look at another facet of this area of your life; it may seem somewhat different when seen from a different point of view." "There is an aspect of your marital problems we have not mentioned, and considering it may put these things in a different light. What do you think your 14-year-old daughter and 12-year-old son think about it?"

Consensual validation is essentially a historical process; by scrutinizing one interpersonal event after another, the therapist and the patient reconstruct the patient's life history. In this process each event has a *present*, a *past* and a *future*. This is true even when discussing something that happened at some point in the patient's earlier years. For example, in discussing an incident which occurred five years previously, three questions arise: (1) What, in all its details and as seen from diverse points of view, happened *at that time?* (2) What things occurred *before that incident* which led up to it? (3) What happened *after that* as a result of it?

Consideration of each interpersonal event in terms of its *present*, *past* and *future* is illustrated by the following three sets of questions.

The Present. "Let's try to reconstruct exactly what happened when you went to your parents' home last Christmas. What occurred on that day to make you feel desolate, lonely and impotently angry?"

The Past. "During your childhood and adolescence what sorts of things usually happened on Christmas? What went on between you and your parents, and what emotional impacts did these things have on you?"

The Future. "How do you think you will handle this annual event next year? Have we learned anything that will help you understand more and suffer less in it?"

For purposes of clear presentation, much material is condensed into each of these three questions. In actual therapy each of these questions would probably be broken into several inquiries, and they would be separated by dialogues that, in their totality, might occupy up to several interviews.

In another technique occasionally employed for consensual validation, the therapist does something to disturb the interpersonal field; to test his hypothesis he deliberately mobilizes anxiety and its concomitant security operations. This should be done *only by an experienced therapist*, and he should know his patient well. He must foresee how he (1) can resolve, or at least much reduce, the anxiety he mobilizes before the interview terminates and (2) can make this a truly therapeutic experience for the patient.

This procedure is shown in the following abridged dialogue.

Therapist: You mentioned a few weeks ago that one of your husband's coworkers is going to England for three months to supervise installation of some new machinery there. Let's suppose that at the last minute this man cannot go and your husband must take his place. How would you feel if this were to occur?

Patient: I'd be pretty upset; I feel I couldn't stand it right now. Just thinking about it makes me tense.

Therapist: What do you mean by "upset" and "tense"?

Patient: Scared, I guess. I couldn't cope with anything that went wrong. What would I do if one of the kids got very sick, or if there were money problems, or if the kids began to get out of hand, or if there were any trouble with his family or mine? I couldn't stand it. I always rely on Tom when anything goes wrong.

Therapist: What do you mean when you say you "couldn't stand it"?

Patient: I don't know. Well, I guess I mean that I'd crack up, or something like that.

Therapist: What do you see yourself as doing, or being like, when you "crack up"?

Patient: I wouldn't be able to go on. I'd just sit around like a zombie and do nothing, or cry all the time, or panic and go all to pieces. Maybe I'd end up in a hospital, or something like that. Everything would get out of control. Just thinking about it makes me pretty upset.

Therapist: In other words, you feel you'd become completely inadequate as a person and might well be mentally and physically incapacitated?

Patient: Yes, something like that.

Therapist: From what I know of you, I feel sure these dreaded things would not happen. Nevertheless, what steps would you take to prevent these terrifying things?

Patient: I'd have to get somebody in to stay with me.

Therapist: Who, for instance?

Patient: I think Barbara would come. She's divorced and has no kids, and she isn't working right now. I think she'd stay with me for three months until Tom got back.

Therapist: And what would Barbara do?

Patient: She and I would talk over anything that went wrong and decide what to do.

Therapist: And what would you do if you decided on a course of action and it failed?

Patient: They we'd try something else. At any rate I'd know that it hadn't gone wrong because I made a bad decision.

Therapist: In other words the situation would be more tolerable for you if you could share the blame and the guilty feelings over poor decisions and failures with Barbara, or even, in your mind at least, put the whole blame on her?

Patient: Well, I guess so. If I made some bad decisions and things went seriously wrong, I don't think I could stand it. It would seem to be the final proof that I'm really not much good for anything.

Therapist: [*Using this to validate a hypothesis* (*tentative interpretation*) *he and the patient have been working on in various interpersonal contexts*]. Is this one more situation in which responsibility panics you because you fear it will prove you are utterly inadequate as a person?

Patient: I guess so. Just thinking of Tom going away frightens me.

Therapist: [*Pointing out the patient's security operation*]. And do we find you once more seeking someone to make your decisions for you and to shoulder the blame and guilt for anything that goes wrong, so you can keep your self-esteem intact?

Patient: I believe that's what I've always done, in one way or another. My nightmare is that someday I'll face a crisis with no one around to help me, and everything will fall apart.

Therapist: [*Taking steps to reduce the anxiety he has mobilized*]. I think it's been useful for us to examine this imaginary situation. It shows that these panicky feelings, which we've seen in your childhood and adolescent experiences, still gnaw at you. However, it's important to emphasize once more that these are *fears*; whenever you have faced a life situation in which you had to shoulder some responsibility, you've managed to do it reasonably well, though it's been very painful for you. You've never "cracked up," and I've seen no evidence that indicates you have much chance of "cracking up" in these situations, though you suffer much in going through them. Moreover, as we've seen, there's little chance your husband would ever be sent out of the country on a job assignment; his kind of work keeps him tied down here. Nevertheless, I think we've learned something in examining your fears, and your speculations on what you'd do about them if this *imaginary* situation arose.

The difference between presenting a hypothesis (tentative interpretation) and making a declarative interpretation (as is commonly done in many other forms of psychotherapy) is contrasted in the following examples. In presenting a hypothesis for consensual validation the therapist says, "Do you think you perhaps are unduly dependent on your parents?" In a positive, declarative interpretation the therapist says, "You are unduly dependent on your parents." The first presentation opens a topic for exploration; the second tends to give the patient a statement which he can accept, or reject or ignore.

Timing is important in presenting a hypothesis for consensual validation. The therapist should put forward a hypothesis for exploration only when he feels he has sufficient information about the patient to guide him in seeking its validation. He also must be able to evaluate the patient's probable emotional reactions to the tentative interpretation. A premature, quite erroneous interpretation may mislead the patient, or puzzle him or make him feel that the therapist has little grasp of what he is suffering. On the other hand, an unduly delayed interpretation may come at a time when its maximal usefulness is long past.

The questions which the therapist should ask himself in timing the presentation of a hypothesis are: (1) Do I have sufficient information to frame this hypothesis in a sound way? (2) Do I know enough about this person to explore this tentative interpretation in various areas of his interpersonal life? (3) Do I understand him well enough to gauge the amount of anxiety this hypothesis may arouse in him? (4) Have I considered alternative hypotheses which may explain the available data equally well?

If the answer to any of these questions is no, the therapist should probably get more information before presenting his hypothesis.

A hypothesis, or tentative interpretation, which has been put forward for consensual validation is available to the patient in the many hours between his treatment sessions to evaluate what is going on in his life. He can use it to see his interpersonal relationships in a new light. The work of consensual validation thus spreads from the treatment periods into the patient's day-to-day life.

OTHER ASPECTS OF CONSENSUAL VALIDATION

Because it requires systematic testing of all hypotheses about what went on in the patient's life, consensual validation does not allow a therapist to cling to theoretical prejudices

about what he thinks *ought* to be wrong with the patient.
Theories must always give way to clinical facts. Interpersonal
psychiatry hence may be uncomfortable for therapists who
have large intellectual and emotional investments in various
psychiatric systems. On the other hand, Sullivan's interpersonal psychiatry is challenging to therapists who do not have
this difficulty.

In general, consensual validation requires verification of a
hypothesis a number of times in diverse settings of the patient's life before it becomes firmly established. In many cases,
the first few times a hypothesis is substantiated in therapy the
patient loses much of what he has gained when the interview
terminates and he returns to the anxiety-laden relationships
of his daily life. When we say the patient "loses" what he
gained, we mean that it is still too painful for him to be *continually* aware of it; it passes outside his field of awareness
and is not available to him as understood, assimilated
experience.

As an interview comes to an end, a patient may use a
variety of maneuvers to brush aside something new and painful which he and the therapist have explored during the
session. For example, he may inquire, "Are we getting anywhere?" or he may relapse into complaints that his symptoms
are no better, or he may digress into a short flight of meaningless verbosity on some insignificant point. On such occasions the therapist may say, "I think we have done useful
work today. We have talked about some distressing, but significant things. We shall probably have to look at these
things a number of times from various points of view before
they become entirely comfortable and meaningful for you."

Sullivan emphasizes that complete consensual validation
about all aspects of a patient's life is an ideal goal which in
practice can never be reached. Each person's interpersonal relationships are too varied and many-faceted to allow absolute

consensual validation. The patient and the therapist can only work until a reasonably high degree of certainty is reached about a number of the patient's main difficulties and there is significant improvement in his emotional and interpersonal functioning. The criteria for satisfactory consensual validation are practical ones: Have these new insights been assimilated into the patient's ways of feeling, thinking and interacting with people? Is his spectrum of awareness now sufficiently broad to permit him to live a comfortable, gratifying life and to adjust to the opportunities and challenges he encounters in it?

Chapter 6

Dynamisms

Sullivan points out that the concepts of many schools of psychiatry are based on metaphors taken from Newton's mechanical concepts of the universe. For example, Freudian psychoanalysis divides the mind into three spatial divisions— the id, the ego and the superego. Forces from one area impinge on another, producing various kinds of feelings and thoughts. Thus, if a force (often represented by a vector arrow) goes from the id upward into the ego, the patient feels anxiety, and if a force travels from the superego down into the ego he feels guilt. Vector arrows crisscrossing between the ego and the space outside the mind indicate the interaction of the ego with the person's environment. These concepts have been somewhat modified and have become more intricate with the development of ego psychology in recent decades, but the fundamental assumptions on which they are based have not been changed.

Sullivan feels this is an artificial, inaccurate way to think about interpersonal relationships and emotional functioning. He also points out that there is no objective, scientifically sound way for proving the validity of these concepts. For example, there is no scientifically valid manner for examining the ego in experiments which any adequately trained person can perform. This general subject has been touched on in previous chapters of this book.

In searching for a better way to explain emotional and interpersonal functioning, Sullivan developed the concept of *dynamisms*.

Dynamisms deal with the transformation and flow of energy. The transformation and flow of energy are more difficult to explain in simple terms than the workings of mechanics. The average person has more difficulty understanding the flow of electricity or the conversion of heat to light than he does in understanding the motions of pulleys, weights and counterweights. Nevertheless, concepts of energy transformation and flow more accurately portray what occurs in human beings and in their interpersonal dealings, for human beings are continually transforming and transmitting energy. In some cases this energy can be measured, and it can be traced from its biochemical and biophysical origins in a person to its expression in interpersonal events; specific examples of this will be given later in this section.

Moreover, Sullivan's concept of dynamisms is more in keeping with the general current of twentieth century scientific thinking to state its principles in terms of the transformation and flow of energy. This, too, is consonant with Sullivan's emphasis on psychiatry as the study of unbroken sequences of interpersonal events, and Sullivan is aware of this added historical dimension of his work.

With this brief preface we may proceed to consider Sullivan's concept of dynamisms and to outline their role in psychotherapy.

A dynamism is a relatively enduring pattern of energy transformation which characterizes the interpersonal relationships and emotional functioning of a person.

The study of any particular dynamism requires

(1) identification of the *source* of its energy and
(2) tracing the *course* of the energy as it flows toward its expression in one or more interpersonal events.

The *source* of a dynamism's energy lies in the biochemical and biophysical nature of a person, and its *course* consists of the transformation and flow of this energy in emotional reactions and in interactions between the person and one or more people around him.

The nature of a dynamism is illustrated in the following two examples; each has been simplified for clarity.

A two-month-old infant experiences the physical sensations that later in life he will know as hunger. These are produced by lowering of his blood sugar, subtle electrolyte changes in his tissues, contractions of his stomach and intestines, and many other things. These constitute the biochemical and biophysical *source* of this dynamism.

Because of these processes the infant becomes physically restless and cries. The energy expressed in these acts alerts his mother; she comes to him, offers him a bottle or her breast and cuddles him as she feeds him. These activities of the mother and the infant involve complex transformations and flows of energy in nervous, hormonal, muscular, emotional and interpersonal ways. Thus, the dynamism which began in biochemical and biophysical tension in the infant ended in an interpersonal event, the affectionate nursing of the infant by his mother; the *course* of the flow of energy in this dynamism has been outlined from its beginning to its conclusion.

The extensive changes which interpersonal life causes in a person during infancy and childhood make the workings of a later dynamism more intricate; tracing the source and course of its energy becomes much more difficult. A seven-year-old child who is arguing at the table with his mother about what he wants for breakfast is involved in a much more complicated process than a two-month-old infant crying for milk. Though the same basic dynamism is still at work, it has been so greatly modified by seven years of interpersonal life that unraveling and understanding it constitute a complex task.

The nature of a dynamism in an adult is outlined in the following example. A 25-year-old woman and a 25-year-old man are working side by side in a business firm. Biochemical processes in the woman create a level of sexual tension in her. This is the *source* of the energy of the ensuing dynamism, which we shall call a *lust dynamism;* this term (discussed in more detail in Chapter 10) is used by Sullivan to designate a dynamism which has as its immediate or possible goal any kind of passionate genital sexual activity.

The woman becomes friendly with the man working beside her and after a series of dates they have sexual intercourse. Thus, a dynamism, proceeding from its physiological *source*, flows through a number of interpersonal activities and finds final expression in a specific kind of interpersonal event. Interpersonal and emotional activities constitute a large part of the dynamism's *course*. As noted above, this dynamism is much simplified, and it is assumed that a similar lust dynamism is operating in the man.

A dynamism, by definition, is typical of the individual in whom it is operating. The ways in which its energy is transformed and flows, and finally is expressed in one or more interpersonal events *are characteristic of the person*. When we say that John is aggressive or that Nancy is affectionate, we are describing in colloquial terms some complex dynamisms that are characteristic of John and Nancy. In conjunction with other things (such as his security operations), a person's dynamisms define him as the individual we know.

The dynamism of the woman described above has been molded by 25 years of life experience. If her interpersonal experiences had been different, she would have had a different kind of dynamism. For example, other kinds of interpersonal relationships during childhood and adolescence might have led her to have a homosexual dynamism; in this case she might have had a homosexual relationship with a woman in her office rather than a heterosexual one with the man working beside her. Complex social, cultural and economic factors also influence the course of a dynamism in many cases. For example, whether or not the affectionate relationship of this woman and man proceeds to sexual intercourse or stops short of it may be influenced by such diverse things as religious beliefs and social ideals.

A dynamism condenses into a single process things which in other psychiatric systems are fragmented. For instance, it embraces the things which in Freudian psychoanalysis are termed instincts, libido, cathexes, defense mechanisms and various other processes. A dynamism emphasizes the unity of emotional and interpersonal functioning.

To cover all human situations, the concept of a dynamism, as given above, must be elaborated somewhat further. After infancy the *source* of the energy of a dynamism is often *interpersonal*. That is, the energy which sets a dynamism in motion is generated by events that occur between people. For example, a parent by his harsh, rejecting behavior produces much smoldering hostility in a child, and this hostility becomes the source of the energy of an ensuing dynamism. In another instance, an adolescent is brutally criticized by others and his feelings of inadequacy and worthlessness constitute the source of energy that sets a dynamism in motion. However, these apparently interpersonal origins of a dynamism are, in the final analysis, biochemical and biophysical. A person can experience hostility, or affection, or low self-esteem only because of complex biochemical and biophysical events which occur in his brain and other body systems. For example, each human thought and feeling require that millions of sodium and potassium ions rapidly travel to and fro across the semipermeable membranes of nerve fibers; innumerable other biochemical events occur simultaneously. Thus, when we say that the source of a dynamism is interpersonal, we are merely describing the aspect of it that we can see in our relationship with another person and the part of it that we can deal with in psychotherapy.

A dynamism may be healthy or unhealthy. Sullivan sometimes couples the word dynamism with the name of the sick process; thus, he speaks of the obsessional dynamism, the schizophrenic dynamism, the paranoid dynamism, and others.

In psychotherapy the patient and the therapist are almost constantly elucidating the unhealthy dynamisms which bring the patient to treatment. They explore the patient's unhealthy patterns of living. The goal is for the patient to abandon sick dynamisms and to substitute healthy ones in their places.

AN EXAMPLE OF THE CONSENSUAL VALIDATION OF A DYNAMISM IN PSYCHOTHERAPY

To illustrate the resolution of a dynamism in psychotherapy we shall examine the case of a patient with an obsessive neurosis.* In order to make the later patient-therapist dialogues clear, a thumbnail sketch of this type of obsessive difficulty will be given in the following three paragraphs.

This kind of problem occurs mainly in mothers between the ages of 25 and 40. It consists of a panic-ridden, obsessive dread that they may murder their children. (It must be em-

---

* The particular type of obsessive difficulty which we shall discuss is one that I have experience in treating; over the years I have collected about 35 cases of this kind of disorder and have published material on it (Archives of General Psychiatry, Volume 1, 12-16, July, 1959 and pages 136 and 141 in Chapman, A. H., Davis, J. M. and Almeida, E. M., *Textbook of Clinical Psychiatry: An Interpersonal Approach*, Second Edition, Philadelphia, J. B. Lippincott, 1976).

phasized that these mothers have no *urge* to kill their children, but rather an obsessive *dread* that in a moment of lost self-control they may do so; women who have true urges to kill their children have other kinds of psychiatric pictures, and their psychodynamics are quite different.) This obsessive preoccupation with infanticide usually is coupled with an obsessive dread of incipient psychosis. The two obsessions complement each other; the patients fear that ideas of murdering their children are so bizarre that they must be signs of actual or imminent psychosis, and that a suddenly full-blown psychosis will at any moment unleash infanticidal acts by them.

These women suffer acutely. Many of them cannot bear to go near the cabinets in which kitchen utensils and knives are kept, for fear the impulse may overtake them when sharp instruments are near at hand. Often they dread to pick up a paring knife for simple kitchen chores, for fear that once they have a potentially fatal instrument in hand they will irresistibly be drawn to harm their children. They live in constant fear of "losing control"; to them "loss of control" is synonymous with psychosis and commission of the murderous act. They envision themselves as continually on the verge of "going berserk" and "running amok." They view themselves as fighting a continuous battle to prevent collapse of their self-restraint which, they feel, stands weakly between them and infanticide. I have seen mothers who struggled with these obsessions for several years before they told anyone about them; they feared that revealing their obsessions would lead to immediate, lifelong incarceration in a psychiatric hospital. I have never seen a patient who fitted this clinical category become psychotic, and I have never seen one who harmed her children. They are, as a rule, passive, dependent persons who have great difficulty in being reasonably assertive, even to the extent of exercising moderate discipline over their children.

This clinical picture also may occur in men, but fathers with this difficulty are not commonly seen in practice. In most cases women with this syndrome cannot become overtly angry; they cannot be assertive of their rights and privileges, and often they are dominated by relatives, coworkers and others. Usually these passive, hostility-suppressing patterns originated in relationships with parents who did not tolerate any expression of anger and assertiveness. During childhood and adolescence these women were made to feel intensely guilty about any aggressiveness, and parental love was painfully withdrawn at such times. These patterns of marked guilt and apprehensiveness about assertiveness were carried into late adolescence and adulthood.

This brief outline of this type of clinical problem prepares us to examine the resolution of one facet of such an *obsessive dynamism* by *consensual validation*.

For this purpose we shall divide the following illustrative dialogues into four psychotherapeutic stages. (In clinical practice, of course, psychotherapy can never be so neatly parceled out.)

The patient (a composite patient formed from many whom I have seen) is a 28-year-old married woman with two children, Janice, aged two, and Bryan, aged four. She has had obsessive fears of infanticide and psychosis for four months when she comes for psychotherapy.

The four stages into which we shall separate the exploration of her *obsessive dynamism* are:

1. Identifying the source of the energy which sets her dynamism in motion; this involves examining both current and past interpersonal relationships.

2. Tracing the course of the transformations and flow of energy in her obsessive dynamism.

3. Examining the final expression of the dynamism in one or more interpersonal events.

4. Observing the resolution of this obsessive dynamism by consensual validation of various aspects of the processes outlined in stages 1, 2 and 3.

1. Identifying the Source of the Energy Which Sets the Dynamism in Motion

The energy which puts the patient's dynamism in motion arises in interpersonal conflicts and traumas in both her current life situation and in her childhood and early adolescent relationships.

These sources of emotional energy are examined in the condensed dialogues which follow.

a. Emotional Energy of the Dynamism Which Arises in the Current Life Situation of the Patient

Patient: My fears are strongest about Janice. I feel terrified whenever I have to do anything with her. I have the same fears of harming Bryan, but they're much weaker.

Therapist: Can you think of any reason why your feelings toward Janice might be different from those toward Bryan?

Patient: When Bryan was born, Bill and I were getting along fine. When I got pregnant with Janice a couple of years later, we were having a lot of trouble; we were fighting all the time and I was thinking of getting a divorce. I'd seen a lawyer. Then I found out I was pregnant. I thought of having an abortion, but decided against it. My feelings were all mixed up, but I went ahead and had her.

Therapist: How did you feel about Janice when she was born?

Patient: I felt she was just one more thing chaining me to Bill and our marriage, which was getting continually worse. I guess I resented her. I tried to be affectionate with her, but I just couldn't do it.

Therapist: Would it be fair to say that you almost hated Janice?

Patient: Maybe hatred is too strong a word, but perhaps not. Anyway, I felt very upset and guilty about it. A mother ought not to feel that way about a child. And it was made worse by the fact that she gave me a lot more trouble than Bryan did when he was a baby. She had a lot of colic and she was fussy much of the time. I had to get up three or four times, or more, every night with her.

Therapist: Do you think that perhaps in an indistinct, wordless way she sensed some of the tension between the two of you?

Patient: Maybe. It seemed we were fighting each other from the beginning.

Here the therapist and the patient have identified one aspect (there probably are others which also will be elucidated) of *the emotional energy in the patient's current life situation* which is fueling her obsessive dynamism. It arises out of her hostility and revulsion toward Janice, her profound guilt about these feelings, and the resulting interpersonal conflict between them.

b. *Emotional Energy of the Patient's Dynamism Which Arises Out of Her Earlier Life Experiences*

Patient: My parents always favored my sister Norma when we were growing up. They seemed to feel that everything she did was right and everything I did was wrong. If Norma argued about something, she always got what she wanted. If I argued I usually was told that I didn't appreciate what my parents were doing for me, that I was upsetting them and making them sick, that nobody could stand to live with me, and that no one could love, or even like, a child who was as awful as I was. I always gave in and did what they wanted; I figured I was such a mess that I didn't deserve anything more than I got. I felt I had to try extra hard in everything I did to get people to like me, or at least to put up with me. If people were irritable with me, or uninterested in me, it seemed like confirmation of everything my parents said.

Therapist: Do you think that underneath all this you had a great deal of resentment, even some hatred, toward your parents?

Patient: I didn't know it then, but I can see now that I probably did. My mother was always telling me to wipe that sullen look off my face, and I kept saying that I wasn't sullen; however, I guess there was more anger inside me than I knew about.

In this abbreviated dialogue the therapist and the patient trace *a second source of energy* that sets the patient's obsessional dynamism in motion; this one, in contrast to the previous one, is in her *past* interpersonal relationships. Sullivan feels that each obsessional patient, in addition to current emotional turmoil, suffered massive depreciation from a hostile parent, or parents. Much lingering fury in the patient, as well as intense feelings of guilt and unworthiness about the hostility he felt toward his parents, provides a second source of energy for his obsessive neurosis. (We are here presenting a simplified version of Sullivan's views on the causes of an obsessional dynamism; our primary aim is to illustrate the functioning of a dynamism and its resolution by consensual validation in psychotherapy.)

2. Tracing the Course of the Transformation and Flow of Energy in the Patient's Obsessive Dynamism

The next step of the patient and the therapist is to follow the transformations and flow of this energy into her obsessive fears of harming her children; in this their attention is primarily on Janice since the patient's obsessive fears center mainly on her. The production of the patient's obsessive dread of psychosis, which is coupled to her fear of infanticide, is also explored.

Patient: I still have my constant dread that at any moment I'll lose my self-control and do something awful to Janice. I can't get that terror out of my head.

Therapist: Does it seem that a sudden tidal wave of hatred will, without warning, sweep you into a vicious act against her?

Patient: I guess so. I've never really been able to love Janice. I've always had to force myself to do anything for her. When she was a baby, changing her diapers and feeding her were hard for me. I felt like shaking her when she wouldn't take her bottle and when I had to get up with her for any reason during the night.

Therapist: Putting my last question in somewhat different words, does it perhaps seem that your resentment against her threatens at any minute to erupt in the most extreme form of hostile expression, killing her?

Patient: I think . . . maybe . . . it's something like that.

Therapist: And, I think you're ready to put it into words now, it's only a short step from such thoughts to feelings that you'd be much freer to break up your unhappy marriage if she were not alive.

Patient: That idea gnaws at me all the time. It makes me feel awful.

Therapist: What do you mean by "awful"?

Patient: Inhuman, worthless, guilty.

Therapist: And yet, as we've seen, such thoughts are common in mothers who have children who have chained them to bad marriages. And in some of these mothers such painful thoughts and feelings fuel panicky, persistent fears that any moment they may pick up a paring knife or some other kind of household utensil and be swept into the act they constantly dread. It's a painful burden to carry around.

Patient: I've been living with it for four months now.

Therapist: Do you feel that a mother who has such thoughts running through her head must be psychotic, or constantly on the brink of becoming so?

Patient: Such thoughts aren't normal. No mother in her right mind would think such things.

Therapist: Would it surprise you to know that I've seen quite a few mothers with exactly the same thing you have, coupled fears of harming their children and becoming insane?

Patient: And what happened to them?

Therapist: When we found out where their feelings of hostility toward their children came from, and explored them at length, all of them improved a lot; most of them in time got rid of their fears entirely. In one way or another, most of them were struggling with problems similar to those you have.

In actual clinical practice this dialogue would, of course, be expanded to occupy at least one or two interviews; it is here condensed to illustrate the basic processes we are discussing. In it we see how the therapist *traces the transformations and flow of the patient's emotional energy into the production of her obsessive symptoms.*

We have so far dealt only with the transformations and

flow of emotional energy generated *in current life experiences*. We shall now outline how emotional energy rising out of turbulent childhood interpersonal relationships undergoes transformations and flows into the production of this patient's obsessive symptomatology.

Therapist: Can you think of any other period in your life when you had panicky, guilt-ridden thoughts that you would be better off if someone were dead?

Patient: When I was a child I sometimes had daydreams of both my parents dying in a car accident. Then I'd go to live with my uncle and aunt, who were very fond of me.

Therapist: And how did you feel about such daydreams?

Patient: At first I felt all right about them, but afterward I felt bad.

Therapist: What do you mean by "bad"?

Patient: Guilty, and sort of scared. I was afraid God would punish me for thinking such things, and that something awful would happen to me because of them. I guess I stopped having those daydreams, or thoughts, when I was about nine or ten years old.

Therapist: Did you sometimes feel that in some strange way your daydreams might actually cause your parents to die in a car accident, or in some other manner?

Patient: Something like that. I remember that once when they both went to a business convention in Chicago I was very upset the whole time they were gone, and I cried a lot. I was convinced they'd die in an accident of some kind, and that somehow I'd feel responsible.

Therapist: Then this is not the first time in your life that you've been troubled by panicky, guilty thoughts about a close person dying because of something you did, or might do?

Patient: No, I guess not. I recall that when I was in the third grade I used to cry myself to sleep every night thinking that my parents might die, and that in some mixed up way I would be the cause of it.

Therapist: When you think about it, were these childhood fears really much different from those you now have about Janice?

In this abridged dialogue the transformations and flow of emotional energy from the patient's past have been followed into the formation of the obsessive fears that bring her to psychotherapy. There are, of course, other sources of emotional energy in her past that contribute to her obsessive disorder; for illustrative purposes, only one such source is considered here.

3. *Examining the Final Expression of the Dynamism in One or More Interpersonal Events*

The patient's obsessive thoughts affect her relationship with Janice and, to a lesser extent, with her son Bryan. These thoughts alter the nature of the interpersonal events that occur between her and them.

Therapist: Do you think your fears of harming Janice, and to a lesser extent Bryan, have affected your relationships with them? Have they influenced the ways in which you get along with them?

Patient: My husband says I can't handle them anymore. He says I let them do anything they want, and never put limits on what they do or discipline them. He says they're becoming a couple of spoiled brats.

Therapist: Is it because you're afraid that if you do anything firm with they you will, as you see it, overshoot the mark and "lose control," and then be swept into the violent acts against them which you fear so much?

Patient: Yes, I'm afraid to do anything with them. I can't control either of them anymore. They do whatever they want.

Therapist: And as Janice and Bryan become more uncontrolled and demanding, do your feelings of helpless anger against them increase still more?

Patient: I almost can't stand to be around them. I can't get close to them anymore. I just do whatever they want to keep peace in the house. I can see that it's no good for them and it's no good for me. It's upsetting Bill more and more, and our marriage is getting steadily worse.

The patient and the therapist have now traced the dynamism *to its final expression in interpersonal events* between the patient and her children, and between the patient and her husband. There are, of course, other interpersonal events in which this dynamism finds expression; we have indicated only a few of them. In addition, as seen here, the sick interpersonal events which the dynamism causes set other unhealthy processes in motion; this is a frequent result of an unhealthy dynamism.

4. *Resolving the Dynamism by Consensual Validation, Which Includes the Processes Outlined in the Three Previous Stages*

The resolution of this obsessive dynamism has, of course, already begun in the dialogues outlined above. In actual psychotherapy there is no neat division between these stages. Two or three of them often are going on at the same time. At every step hypotheses are advanced and their consensual validation is, bit by bit, carried out.

In the following dialogue a hypothesis (tentative interpretation) concerning yet another facet of the patient's obsessive disorder is put forward, and initial moves toward its consensual validation are begun.

Therapist: You have often mentioned your fear of "losing control" and doing something dreadful. Exactly how do you envision yourself when you think of "losing control"?

Patient: I'd simply go berserk. I'd not be able to stop myself from doing terrible things, and might not even know what I was doing.

Therapist: In other words, is one of your basic fears that your control of yourself is so weak that it is constantly on the verge of collapsing?

Patient: I feel that all the time I'm just holding on by my fingertips. If I let go I'll fall into the abyss.

Therapist: [*Here condensing things that in actual therapy would be spread over much more time*]. Would it surprise you to learn that this is not really one of your problems, and that in reality one of your major difficulties is that you exercise far too much control over yourself? And that you bottle up many kinds of feelings too much and, after roundabout courses, they come out as these persistent, panicky fears? Do you think that if you could be more comfortable with your feelings of anger, resentment and guilt toward Janice and others you might be a lot better off? Is it possible that if you could get comfortably angry with Janice and Bryan when they deserve it, and let them know about it clearly, you would begin to discharge some of the emotional turbulence that is producing your fears? And that, in addition, you have this same basic problem in many other areas of your life, and that comfortable, guiltless assertiveness would help you in many other kinds of interpersonal relationships?

Patient: It would be hard to do.
Therapist: If it were easy, you would not have had to come
to see me.

The patient and the therapist have started on a long process
of testing the validity of the hypotheses the therapist has put
forward. Such validation will involve detailed examination of
many interpersonal events in the patient's current and past
life. More hypotheses will in time be advanced as psychotherapy proceeds, and they too will undergo consensual validation as the patient's obsessional dynamism is gradually
resolved.

An explanatory note is necessary regarding the illustrative
dialogues we are using. As will be discussed in Chapter 8,
Sullivan emphasizes that each therapist gradually acquires a
repertory of therapeutic techniques which work best for him.
No two therapists would handle this dynamism in exactly the
same way. The therapeutic steps outlined in these abridged
dialogues inevitably reflect my own techniques, based as
closely as possible on Sullivan's methods. In addition, all psychotherapy looks a little flat and artificial when put on paper;
it comes to life and becomes more convincing when it
is accompanied by the vocal intonations, gestures, facial expressions and other nonverbal activities of both the therapist
and the patient. Nevertheless, I believe that brief illustrative
dialogues, with all their shortcomings, give a much clearer
idea of the nature of psychotherapy than mere descriptions
of it in didactic prose.

Chapter 7

Parataxic Distortions in Therapy and in Daily Life

Sullivan took both the term and the concept of *parataxic distortions* from the work of the American psychologist and psychiatrist Thomas V. Moore. Moore typifies the individuality of many American psychiatrists during the first three decades of this century. He was ordained a Catholic priest in 1901, received his medical degree from Johns Hopkins in 1915, and thereafter specialized in psychiatry. He was intermittently active, first as a psychologist and then as a psychiatrist, in the Washington-Baltimore area from 1903 to 1924. Sullivan, who worked in the Washington-Baltimore area from early 1922 onward, knew him during the last two years of this period. In 1924 Moore joined the Benedictine order and retired from clinical work; he died in a monastery in northern Spain in 1969 at the age of 91. He today would probably be forgotten in psychiatry had not Sullivan adopted his concept of parataxic distortions. Sullivan was always careful in his lectures and writings to note his indebtedness to Moore, to whom he sometimes referred by his Benedictine title of Dom Thomas V. Moore.

A. PARATAXIC DISTORTIONS IN THE PATIENT-THERAPIST RELATIONSHIP

THE PRINCIPLE OF PARATAXIC DISORDERS

Before considering the role of parataxic disorders in psychotherapy it is necessary to outline their broader characteristics, since they occur in many kinds of interpersonal relationships.

A parataxic distortion occurs when an individual deals with another person as if he were someone else, usually a close person from the individual's past interpersonal life.

The nature of a parataxic distortion is made clear in the following example. Throughout childhood and adolescence a girl is reared by a cold, controlling mother, and she fights chronically against her mother's harsh domination. At college and in work situations this girl later finds herself in frequent conflicts with women supervisors and other authoritative women with whom she has prolonged contact. Even mild directions from older women evoke resistance and irritability in her. In this *parataxic distortion* this girl is dealing with all older, supervisory women *as if they were her mother*. Neither the girl nor the women with whom she comes in conflict understand the determinants of her behavior.

In his last years Sullivan widened the concept of parataxic distortions to embrace *all types of interpersonal events in which a person's feelings and behavior are warped by the effects of unhealthy relationships with close persons earlier in his life.*

Parataxic distortions occur to at least a minor extent in the daily lives of all people. Each person carries into many kinds of interpersonal relationships a few unhealthy tendencies which are the products of undesirable features of his close relationships during his childhood and adolescence. If these parataxic distortions are small and do not cause significant problems, they may be considered within normal limits. If they are major and cause appreciable difficulties in daily life, they are clearly unhealthy. If they are severe, we say that the person has a psychiatric disorder.

The objection is sometimes raised that Sullivan's concept of parataxic distortions is merely Freud's concept of transference decked out in new words. Persons who make such objections have not read Sullivan carefully and do not understand fully the nature of parataxic distortions. Newton and Einstein both used the concept (and the term) of gravity, but Einstein's principle of gravity is quite different from that of Newton. The same is true of Freud's concept of transference and Sullivan's principle of parataxic distortions. Since the emphasis of this book is on psychotherapeutic techniques, we cannot consider in detail the differences between transference and parataxic distortions and illustrate these differences in clinical examples. However, in the following paragraphs some basic dissimilarities will be outlined.

Firstly, Freud considers transference, especially in psychotherapy, to be *an emotional reliving* of a former traumatic experience. Sullivan feels that no one ever relives anything, either in therapy or outside it. In a parataxic distortion a person does not *relive* an experience, but merely tends to repeat a pattern of feeling and behavior which he developed gradually during his formative years.

Secondly, Freud feels that in prolonged therapy a patient *always* develops toward the therapist feelings he had about a close person, almost invariably a parent, during the first seven years of his life. By reliving this experience in his relationship with the therapist over a prolonged period, the patient is felt to be freed of unhealthy consequences of that relationship. Sullivan feels that this does not occur. A patient merely brings into his relationship with the therapist patterns of living he previously has developed. For example, a person who is ingratiating toward everyone is ingratiating toward the therapist, and a person who is aggressive in his interpersonal relationships tends to be aggressive toward the therapist. An individual does not develop a new personality as he enters the therapist's office. Examination of how the patient feels and behaves in his relationship with the therapist is often a useful procedure since the patient-therapist relationship as a rule is the only one which is available for direct, on-the-spot scrutiny. This is much different from saying that a patient *relives* something in the few hours per week or per month that he spends in the therapist's office.

Thirdly, Freud states that detailed, prolonged analysis of the patient-therapist relationship (transference analysis) is always necessary in psychotherapy, except when its goals are superficial and limited. Transference analysis often occupies over half the time in a course of Freudian psychoanalysis. Freud makes transference analysis one of the three criteria for determining whether a course of psychotherapy truly conforms to his principles (the other two criteria are use of the concepts of childhood sexuality and the unconscious mind). Sullivan is much more flexible about examination of patient-therapist parataxic distortions in psychotherapy; it may or may not be important in any particular case. Many patients get well in psychotherapy without dealing with parataxic phenomena in the patient-therapist relationship. When parataxic distortions are marked in therapy and can be fruitfully employed, the therapist uses them, but in many cases examination of them is not necessary.

Sullivan recognizes that many complex things occur in the patient-therapist relationship. Merely discussing his life problems with an interested, helpful professional person is often an important ingredient of the therapeutic process. Catharsis of one's feelings in the presence of an individual who is neither shocked, nor censorious, nor oversolicitous is frequently useful, regardless of the therapist's theoretical orientation. In many cases these factors do not fall neatly into the category of either transference phenomena or parataxic elements; they are simply nonspecific products of the special kind of interpersonal relationship that occurs in psychotherapy.

THE HANDLING OF PARATAXIC DISTORTIONS IN THERAPY

During psychotherapy a patient and a therapist may deal with two kinds of parataxic distortions:

(1) Those that occur in the patient's relationship with the therapist and

(2) those that are going on in the patient's life situations or have occurred in his past.

An example of the first type occurs if the patient attempts to manipulate and control the therapist by trying to make him feel inadequate and guilty about alleged lack of improvement in therapy. An example of the second type occurs if the patient manipulates and controls his marital partner and children by making them feel inadequate and guilty in many kinds of situations.

We shall in this section discuss how to handle parataxic distortions that occur in the patient-therapist relationship. In the second half of this chapter we shall consider how to deal with parataxic distortions that occur elsewhere in the patient's life.

As noted in the preceding section, examination of parataxic distortions in the patient-therapist relationship is not an imperative feature of a course of psychotherapy. In many cases of successful psychotherapy, patient-therapist parataxic distortions are never investigated. Study of many aspects of the patient's important past and current interpersonal relationships may be more profitable than scrutiny of the one he has with the therapist.

Exploration of parataxic distortions in the patient-therapist relationship also varies much from one type of psychiatric disorder to another. Patients with various kinds of emotional problems differ in their capacity to tolerate the anxiety aroused by such investigations. For example, a person with a passive personality disorder usually tolerates it well, but a schizoid or schizophrenic patient may be panicked into silence or abandonment of therapy by examining parataxic disturbances in his relationship with the therapist. Attempts to evaluate parataxic phenomena with severely depressed patients usually are fruitless, whereas they often are valuable in work with obsessional patients.

A parataxic distortion that occurs in psychotherapy has occurred many times previously in the patient's life. The passive patient has had passive parataxic distortions in many of his relationships since childhood, and the aggressive individual has likewise repeated his parataxic pattern in many interpersonal situations. However, the patient's parataxic experience in therapy differs in a crucial way from all his previous parataxic experiences in everyday life. In all other relationships the patient aroused strong emotions and reactions in the people whom he involved in his parataxic distortions. People liked him or disliked him, exploited him or submitted to him, sought him out or shunned him, and had many other kinds of reactions to his parataxically determined acts.

The therapist, in contrast, offers the patient a special kind of interpersonal relationship, since he does not react emotionally to parataxic behavior and his feelings toward the patient are not changed by it. He merely regards the patient's parataxic distortion as a potentially useful thing to examine in helping the patient to solve his emotional problems. This is one of the features of the patient-therapist relationship which makes it truly unique in the patient's life.

Patient: I'm having trouble finding things to talk about. There doesn't seem to be much to discuss anymore.

Therapist: Do you sometimes wonder what my reaction will be if our sessions begin to drag?

Patient: Well, yes. I figure you may get tired of all this and make our interviews less frequent, or terminate the treatment altogether. That sort of scares me.

Therapist: In other words, you're afraid I'll get rid of you if you don't perform as you're supposed to?

Patient: I guess so. That possibility worries me.

Therapist: Can you think of other situations in your life in which you feared that failure to do what you were supposed to do would lead to someone rejecting you?

The therapist has here used an incipient parataxis to direct the patient's attention to similar parataxic experiences elsewhere in his life. After exploring several such parataxes, he may return (in the same interview or several interviews later) to the patient's parataxic distortion in the interview situation.

Therapist: And so you feel that I, like these other people in your life, may think badly of you and discard you if you don't perform as you should?

Patient: I guess that's about it.

Therapist: It's almost as if I'd ceased being your therapist and had become someone else, such as your mother who rejected you when you didn't do as she wanted, or your husband who becomes cold and sullen when you can't do as he wishes. Does it, in a sense, seem as if I'd stopped being your therapist and had become just one more rejecting person in your life? Is it the old failure occurring again, or threatening to occur?

Patient: I don't like to look at it that way. However, I think that's more or less how I feel.

Therapist: Then maybe we can learn something by examining how you feel and what you fear in the situation which is going on right now in this office.

Sullivan has a striking way of talking about patient-therapist parataxic distortions. He states that at these points in therapy three people are involved: (1) the parataxically distorted, "imaginary" therapist, (2) the patient, who is interacting with this "illusory" therapist, and (3) the actual participant-observing therapist, who is seeking to identify whom the parataxically distorted therapist represents.

The therapeutic task is to discover who the parataxically distorted therapist really is; he represents someone from the past who had an unhealthy, close interpersonal relationship with the patient and in it molded his interpersonal functioning into sick patterns.

Therapist: Would you agree that you're becoming impatient and irritable with me?

Patient: Well, everything here seems to annoy me. I feel almost as if I'd like to blow up and tell you off.

Therapist: Do you feel I've done something, or have omitted to do something, that has caused this irritability?

Patient: No, you're no different than you've always been. I guess it's me.

Therapist: Old interpersonal patterns sometimes crop up in the relationship between a patient and a therapist. Does it seem, in a sense, almost as if I've become someone else, some close person in your past toward whom you felt this same kind of resentment and hostility?

Patient: A couple of people come to mind.

Therapist: Let's talk about them. Maybe we can find out where this irritability comes from.

A parataxic distortion directs attention to two things: (1) It illustrates some aspect of how the patient interacts with people in his day-to-day living and (2) it focuses attention on the historic precedent for this pattern in the patient's past life. Each parataxic distortion is, in a way, an effort to communicate something on these two levels of experience, and the therapist's task is to find out what it is.

Patient: My irritability is beginning to make this treatment difficult. It's harder to talk than it was. It's even getting harder to come here.

Therapist: Your irritability does cause problems, but it also gives us an opportunity. You have a chance to look back into your past and find out why you developed this pattern of becoming hostile toward each person with whom you have prolonged, close contact. In the relationship here in this office, and only here, you can be sure that the other person will not become upset and retaliatory because of your irritability. He will merely work with you to try to discover this ghost from your past whom you find in many people around you.

As a rule, investigation of parataxic distortions in the patient-therapist relationship comes late in therapy, if at all. A patient must feel fairly secure in his relationship with the therapist before he can examine parataxic disturbances in it.

Unmasking a parataxic distortion often precipitates anxiety; the patient in many cases fears that it will either break up therapy or will convert it into an uncomfortable, conflictive process. In addition, the patient frequently is afraid to come to grips with a painful relationship from his past in such a graphic, emotionally charged manner. It is one thing to talk about a traumatic interpersonal association in one's past life and another to discuss a painful relationship with the involved person sitting a few feet away.

The patient, therefore, must assume much of the initiative in exploring a patient-therapist parataxic distortion; to do this he must feel that the therapist considers him a sufficiently worthwhile person to merit this investigation, which frequently is stressful and awkward. The therapist cannot push too much. If the patient is unable to do most of the work it usually is best to direct the course of therapy, at least for the time being, into other channels of inquiry.

Some kinds of patients find the first identification of a parataxic distortion an eerie experience. It appears strange to the patient that he has, in a sense, cast the therapist into someone else's role. This tends to occur particularly in schizoid persons, somewhat paranoid individuals, patients with major hysterical disorders, and persons whose hold on reality is weak; it also may disturb individuals whose self-esteem is low. The therapist must intervene actively with such patients to demonstrate that the parataxic distortion "makes sense" and "is reasonable" when seen in the context of the patient's total life history. The therapist emphasizes that the parataxis is an attempt to communicate something, and that it opens new avenues for increasing the patient's understanding of his current and past life experiences.

For example, the therapist may say, "This feeling toward me must arise out of your past history. It is based on an old relationship to a significant person who left a mark on your ways of relating to people. Perhaps you can recollect another relationship in which you had similar feelings and attitudes." Even if the patient cannot immediately make such connections, the therapist's words quell his anxiousness because they make the parataxis seem understandable and logical. This usually allows the inquiry to go on in a useful way.

There is a significant exception to the general tendency for exploration of patient-therapist parataxic distortions to come late in therapy. In some cases the patient's parataxically warped behavior is of such a nature that it causes a major obstacle to therapy at its beginning, and it must be dealt with to some extent to allow therapy to start. For example, a patient may be so anxious not to offend the therapist that he talks only about topics which he feels will gratify the therapist; in his fear of annoying the therapist in some way, he ends up talking only of trivia and irrelevancies. In such instances the therapist, in as simple and gentle a manner as possible, must deal with this parataxically determined behavior if meaningful treatment is to begin at all.

In a situation of this kind the therapist may, *in essence*, say, "You need not be afraid of upsetting me by anything you say. I shall not terminate treatment if you say something which, as you fear, may bother or irritate me. This perhaps is what happened in one or more of your close relationships in the past. Someone important to you treated you that way, and you expect the same thing from me, almost as if I were that person. However, that does not happen here. We merely note such fears as part of the feelings and experiences that we can use in talking about your problems."

In a similar way a therapist may say to a patient whose low self-esteem and feelings of inadequacy are paralyzing therapy from the outset, "Do not mistake me for others. As we have noted, you have long feared that when, as you see it, people discover how inferior and worthless you are they will abandon you in disgust. You perhaps are afraid that if I really get to know you I shall behave in that way. That sort of thing doesn't happen here. We're only interested in finding out where you got these painful, unjustified feelings, and in trying to get rid of them so they will not make you uncomfortable with people."

FACTORS IN THE THERAPIST'S BEHAVIOR WHICH MAY
CONTAMINATE PARATAXIC DISTORTIONS

A therapist at all times is observing *the interpersonal field between the patient and himself*. He understands the patient only by observing what is said and done in that field. He therefore must constantly be aware that his own behavior at times may affect what the patient says and does. Each therapist frequently must consider the possibility that a patient's actions do not constitute a parataxic distortion but are, at least in part, reactions to things he himself has done.

In a simple example, let us assume that a therapist has had a bad morning with his tax accountant and has learned that he owes a sizable sum of money in back taxes which he will have trouble paying at this time; he arrives at his office in a depressed, irritable mood. His first patient is an insecure, passive individual who reacts to the therapist's irritability and depression (betrayed by the therapist's vocal intonations, facial expressions, body postures, and diminished alertness in working with the patient) by becoming apprehensive and silent. The therapist's second patient is a person with strong feelings of inadequacy, and he responds to the therapist's mood by feeling that the therapist has become discouraged with him and may shortly dismiss him from treatment. Other patients during the course of the day react in different untoward ways *to the changes in the interpersonal field produced by the therapist's emotional state*.

This kind of contamination of the interpersonal field is more common in psychotherapy than is sometimes recognized. Therapists, like everyone else, have occasional problems with their marital partners, children and friends, and they also get physically sick; if a therapist is coming down with a bad cold or during the day has a sudden bout of diarrhea, his

alertness and rapport with his patients are likely to be somewhat impaired.

There is no completely satisfactory way to handle these
situations. If the therapist's distress is going to be brief, he can
cancel his appointments for half a day or more, but many
difficulties drag on for days or weeks and it is not feasible
for a therapist to abandon his practice each time he is not
in his best form. This type of difficulty, incidentally, is not
eliminated by treatment situations in which the patient and
the therapist do not face each other. As pointed out previously, the patient has ample opportunity to examine the
therapist at the beginning and end of the hour, and the therapist's mood is transmitted by nonverbal things such as vocal
intonations, physical restlessness, apathy, verbal activity, unusual silences, and many other things to which patients soon
become acutely sensitive.

If a tense or physically uncomfortable therapist retreats
into cautious silence and inactivity until he is feeling better,
he is, in a sense, deceiving his patients since they are left to
feel that therapy is going on in an alert manner when in fact
the therapist has to some extent withdrawn from it. It may be
suggested that the therapist in such cases should get psychotherapeutic help for himself, and perhaps he should; however,
emotional distress in many instances is not so quickly resolved
in treatment that the therapist is immediately restored to a
state in which he no longer contaminates interpersonal fields
between his patients and himself.

The therapist, therefore, must constantly be checking his
feelings and behavior to be sure that he is not disturbing the
interpersonal field. We are *not* at this point discussing the
difficulty that in Freudian psychoanalysis is termed counter-
transference; that is, we are not talking about unfavorable
emotional reactions of the therapist which are caused by sizable personality problems in him. We also are not discussing

reactions of the therapist to what the patient says and does; we are here considering things the therapist brings into the interpersonal field independently of what the patient is doing in it.

What does a therapist do when he faces these kinds of problems?

First of all, he remains constantly attentive to the possible occurrence of such difficulties by virtue of his awareness that the basic question in psychotherapy is not "What is the patient doing?" but rather "What is occurring between him and me?" He focuses continually on *the interpersonal field* between the patient and himself and recognizes it as an important area of therapy.

He then refines the preceding question a step further by asking, "Am I doing anything that is disturbing the interpersonal field? Do these words and actions of the patient constitute a parataxic distortion, or are they reactions to contaminating acts and attitudes I have brought into the interview situation?" The participant-observing therapist vigilantly observes himself, as well as the patient and the interactions between the two of them.

Being observantly aware of any tension in himself, the therapist works *in a deliberate manner* to avoid, or correct, any distortions he may cause in the interpersonal field. For example, if an argument earlier that day with his marital partner has left him somewhat irritable, he does all he can to camouflage his annoyance, and he takes into account any influence it may have on the interpersonal field. If he is somewhat depressed because of a serious suicidal attempt by one of his patients the preceding day, he is careful to minimize the expression of his upset and to note any influence it may have in his relationships with his various patients. The participant-observing therapist is able to do this because he is professionally trained to observe himself, the patient and the interpersonal field between them. It is his *professionally trained awareness* which permits him to diminish the effects of any transitory tensions in himself on the treatment process.

In some cases he may point out his limitations to the patient. "I'm coming down with a bad cold; if I seem a little less alert today, it is not a reaction to anything you are doing or saying." "I have been dealing with a few tensions in my own life during the last few days. If you note a tinge of impatience in me it is not caused by anything connected with you." The therapist may also do this in retrospect. "In looking back on our last session I feel that perhaps I was wrong in some of my comments about your relationship with your daughter. I was not feeling well that day, and I think my indisposition may have affected my perceptiveness and judgment. Let's take another look today at the relationship between you and your daughter."

Some therapists feel that admissions of shortcomings and errors by a therapist impair his subsequent effectiveness. They feel that the patient, retreating into a "Physician, heal thyself" stance, may resist and doubt many things the therapist afterward says and does. Sullivan does not feel this way. Patients are not so naive that they expect perfect performances from their therapists; usually they are reassured that they are in the hands of a flexible human being, as well as a person who has expert knowledge of interpersonal relationships and emotional functioning. Moreover, if psychotherapy is an exploration of the patient's life in which many hypotheses are put forward and tested in consensual validation, some hypotheses are bound to be wrong or to need modification as more data are accumulated. The therapist is not an aloof Olympian who hands down infallible pronouncements, and patients know this as well as anyone else.

Up to this point we have been discussing contaminants of the patient-therapist relationship which the therapist brings into the interview *from day-to-day tense events in his personal life*; we have used, as illustrative examples, therapists' reactions caused by financial problems, physical illnesses and discomforts, marital tensions, and other situations.

We shall now examine contaminants introduced into the interview situation by the therapist *in response to things the patient does and says*. For example, we shall consider anxiety, irritability and other untoward reactions produced in therapists by clinging dependence, hostility and other attitudes of patients.

Because of things that patients do and say, every therapist at times becomes anxious during psychotherapy. On such occasions the therapist should do two main things.

Firstly, the *participant-observing* therapist should be aware of his discomfort. He should recognize that something has happened in the interview to make him feel apprehensive, or guilty, or inadequate, or irritable, and he should make a careful survey of what has occurred to mobilize such feelings. In doing this, the therapist learns something about himself. He learns how he reacts to people and what kinds of interpersonal experiences tend to upset him. For example, he may learn that clinging, demanding behavior by a patient (or anyone else in his life) tends to irritate him, or to make him feel inadequate; knowing this, he can more comfortably handle these feelings and is more effective in dealing with such patients. Sullivan feels that anxiety in the therapist, when recognized and dealt with, is an "ally" in therapy. He also feels that the therapist grows to some extent by virtue of such insights and interpersonal adjustments. Though the therapeutic situation is primarily designed to benefit the patient, the therapist often gains new dimensions of emotional and interpersonal health in his work.

Secondly, in recognizing his emotional reactions to the patient, the therapist gets profounder insights into what goes

on between the patient and various other people in his daily
life. For example, the patient who by clinging, demanding
behavior arouses irritability, or guilt, or solicitousness in the
therapist probably mobilizes the same feelings, or kindred
ones, in his marital partner, children, friends and other close
persons by the same behavior. The therapist thus gets clearer
ideas about why the patient's relatives treat him as they do,
and his understanding about what goes on in the patient's
interpersonal relationships becomes broader. In doing this,
the *participant-observing therapist* is, in a sense, converting
the office situation into a laboratory in which the patient's
interpersonal life is studied; in this work the therapist is using
his own personality as an important research instrument.

There are limits to the extent to which a therapist can use
his emotional reactions in this way. The limits are reached
when a therapist cannot become comfortably aware of the
feelings a patient mobilizes in him, or when his feelings are
so strong that they impair his understanding of what is going
on. A therapist who frequently has strong apprehensiveness,
guilt, feelings of inadequacy and other emotional reactions,
and whose therapeutic capacity is marred by such difficulties, needs psychotherapy for himself in order to do good
work. Sullivan, however, is somewhat more flexible than many
psychiatric innovators on the question of whether therapists
routinely require psychotherapy for themselves in order to
be fit for their work. Though psychotherapy for a therapist
is an enriching experience, both personally and professionally,
it is mandatory only when the the therapist has emotional
and interpersonal problems of such degrees that they signifi-
cantly contaminate his relationships with patients and reduce
his therapeutic effectiveness.

When all these facets of doing psychotherapy are frankly
faced, it is clear that it is a very intricate, difficult task. Sullivan states that when a therapist comes to grips with the over-

whelming complexities of his job he realizes how limited his competence must always be, and that any therapist who is exuberantly self-confident, let alone arrogant, about psychotherapy does not know what he is doing.

B. DEALING WITH PARATAXIC DISTORTIONS IN DAILY LIFE

We have so far in this chapter dealt with parataxic distortions that occur in the relationship between the patient and the therapist; now we shall consider parataxic distortions that occur in the patient's day-to-day life with his family, work associates, friends and others. The therapist and the patient spend the bulk of their time discussing these and kindred areas, past and present, in the patient's life.

In preparing to deal with this aspect of psychotherapy, it is first necessary to consider the axiom which Sullivan terms *the tendency toward health*.

PARATAXIC DISTORTIONS AND THE TENDENCY TOWARD HEALTH

A fundamental assumption (and from a scientific point of view it can at present be considered no more than an assumption) in Sullivan's thinking is termed *the tendency toward health*. This axiom states that *in all persons there is a basic tendency toward emotional and interpersonal health, and that each person moves toward such health if he is not obstructed by traumatic feelings and experiences*.

As a result, when unhealthy security operations, parataxic distortions and other hindering difficulties are removed in psychotherapy, the patient spontaneously grows toward emotional health. Thus, when a passive person's anxious feelings about being assertive are removed, he begins to assert himself. In a similar way, the primary problem of a homosexual is not attraction to persons of his own sex but feelings of panic, loathing and inadequacy about genital intimacy with persons of the opposite sex; if these impeding feelings are resolved, he proceeds to make a comfortable heterosexual adjustment. Sullivan employs the following metaphor to make these points clear: The problem in a garden is not the flowers but the weeds; if the weeds are eliminated, the flowers grow in a healthy way.

The tendency toward health cannot be accepted as a scientific principle, since observable, repeatable experiments to prove or disprove it have not been devised. However, there is a certain amount of commonsense evidence in its favor.

This evidence is most easily approached through consideration of facts about human physical functioning. At each moment many millions of chemical and biophysical events occur in each person. An individual, for example, is able to read a sentence in a book only because millions of sodium and potassium ions rapidly crisscross semipermeable linings of nerve fibers in his brain, and in millions of cells in his cerebral cortex intricate chemical reactions take place. The durations of these events are measured in millionths of seconds, and similarly complicated biochemical events are occurring in every organ of the body. When the vast complexity of human physical functioning is considered, it would seem statistically probable, indeed almost inevitable, that something would go drastically wrong each minute in every individual. However, it doesn't. Most people function reasonably well physically most of the time. It therefore is justifiable to summarize these facts by saying that there is in the human body *a basic tendency toward health.*

Sullivan feels that the same principle holds true in emotional and interpersonal functioning. When the intricacies of interpersonal relationships and emotional functioning, as outlined throughout this book, are considered, it would seem statistically probable that severe difficulties would arise constantly in all interpersonal relationships. However, they don't. Most people get along reasonably well with most other people the majority of the time, and they live in a fair degree of emotional comfort. It therefore seems reasonable to summarize these facts in the statement that in human interpersonal life there is *a tendency toward health*, and that things go wrong mainly when this tendency toward health is obstructed. It may be obstructed by sick security operations, parataxic distortions, anxiety and similar impediments.

The tendency toward health in both physical and interpersonal life is presumably the product of millions of years of evolution. If man had not slowly developed a tendency toward physical health, he would long ago have become an extinct species, and if he similarly had not developed a tendency toward interpersonal health, he could not have evolved the complex familial and socioeconomic systems in which he lives. These socioeconomic and cultural systems embrace huge numbers of people, and though they by no means function ideally they operate in such ways that most people live in reasonable degrees of interpersonal comfort a large part of the time.

The tendency toward health works in favor of the patient and the therapist in the psychotherapeutic process. Moreover, because of it, Sullivan says, a therapist is never called on to "cure" anybody. The therapist's task is to work with the patient to remove the obstacles (sick security operations, parataxic distortions, anxiety and others) to his emotional health, and once these hindrances are resolved the patient spontaneously "cures" himself.

A CLINICAL EXAMPLE OF THE TENDENCY TOWARD
HEALTH OPERATING AFTER REMOVAL OF A
PARATAXIC DISTORTION

To illustrate how the tendency toward health operates after removal of a parataxic distortion, I shall outline the case of one of my schizophrenic patients; this presentation is necessarily condensed and simplified in order to cover it in a few pages.

I saw this patient over a three-year period. At the age of 22 she became acutely psychotic in a schizophrenic illness; she was agitated and seclusive, and had paranoid delusions, auditory and visual hallucinations and strong suicidal urges. During the first five months of treatment she was hospitalized twice for approximately two months each time. Afterward she was seen in psychotherapy two or three times each week. She received no phenothiazine or other antipsychotic medication since, among other things, these medications were just being introduced at the time of her illness and were not yet in widespread use. This patient has remained well for 21 years since her treatment ended; I have chosen her for this presentation since I have a long-term follow-up on this case. She has married and has had a successful vocational career. Today, of course, most psychiatrists would employ antipsychotic phenothiazine medication in addition to group or individual psychotherapy and hospital milieu therapy.

The case is mainly presented in dialogues. These are not verbatim from interviews, but are abbreviated samples to illustrate how removal of a parataxic distortion allows the tendency toward health to operate. These dialogues are labeled to indicate four general stages of treatment:

1. Identification and exploration of the basic parataxic distortion.

2. The operation of the parataxic distortion in the patient's day-to-day life.
3. The operation of the parataxic distortion in the patient-therapist relationship.
4. The functioning of the tendency toward health in leading the patient into sound patterns of interpersonal life when the obstructing parataxic distortion is removed.

1. Identification and Exploration of the Basic Parataxic Distortion

Patient: By the time I was seven or eight my life was divided between the store and home; the only other place I spent much time was at school. Right after school I had to go to the store. My parents didn't trust the employees, and I wrapped packages and watched the employees to make sure they didn't sneak out any merchandise when they went out for coffee, or at closing time. When I was nine they put me behind the cash register; only my father, my mother and I were allowed to touch it.

My mother and father fought all the time, both at the store and at home. They screamed at each other and called one another awful names. They did the same thing with me. Every time I did something wrong at the store my father bawled me out in front of the employees and the customers, and my mother yelled at me and threatened to hit me, but she never did.

The store stayed open until 8 o'clock six days a week, and later than that between Thanksgiving and Christmas. We often had dinner brought in from a nearby restaurant. My father said that in our kind of business we were working for nickels and dimes and couldn't miss a single customer. When I went home from the store I studied for a while and then went to bed. I got up early every morning, got my own breakfast and went to school. If I had breakfast with them, they always quarreled with each other, and brought me into it, one way or another. I read books or studied at school until classes began. On Saturdays I worked all day at the store, and on Sundays I got out of the house on one pretext or another; I went to the movies every Sunday afternoon and Sunday night.

Therapist: Was there no one who gave you a little comfortable affection and esteem?

Patient: I guess my parents loved me in their way, but they were always so upset with their own troubles that they couldn't give any affection to me, even when things were a little better for them. The only people I talked to much were the maids we had at home; I used to sit in the kitchen and talk with them while they worked. But none of them ever stayed long; my mother fought with them and they left.

Therapist: What about school? Did you get close to any of the other kids, or to any of the teachers?

Patient: I stayed pretty much to myself. I was sort of afraid of the other kids. I was no good at games, and so I just watched the other kids play. I was afraid they'd laugh at me, and not want me on any of their teams when they found out I couldn't play any of the games very well. I got good grades and the teachers said I was a good student, but I didn't get close to any of them.

Therapist: Did your brother give you much attention?

Patient: He had his own group and didn't have much to do with me; he was six years older than I was. My mother spoiled him. He didn't have to work at the store and he did pretty much what he wanted. My father called him a worthless bum, but gave him money for whatever he wanted. My brother made fun of me all the time, and I stayed out of his way.

Therapist: Was there no one during your childhood and adolescence who gave you the feeling that relationships with people could be pleasant and satisfying?

Patient: When I think about it in those terms, I guess not. All I remember is working at the store, being bawled out, going to school, reading by myself a great deal, getting away from the house as much as I could, and going to the movies a lot. Sometimes I'd sit through the same movie two or three times just to fill up a Sunday or a holiday.

Therapist: Nancy, by the time you reached adolescence, say when you were 13 or 14, what general sorts of things did you feel go on between people, and how did you feel about getting involved with them?

Patient: I suppose I didn't trust anybody, but I never thought about it in those terms.

Therapist: Would it be fair to say you felt that getting close to anybody was dangerous, a thing to be avoided at any cost?

Patient: I guess so. If people tried to get friendly with me, I avoided them. I don't believe I ever put it into words, but I think I felt that once you got involved with anybody you never got free; it was just endless quarreling and fighting after that, and in the end it left you feeling awful, like dirt, no good.

Therapist: Was it like getting caught in a trap?

Patient: Yes, something like that.

In this dialogue (which contains material condensed from many interviews) the patient and the therapist identified and explored a parataxic distortion. Because of the painfulness of her important interpersonal relationships during childhood and adolescence, the patient developed strong feelings that all close interpersonal associations were agonizing traps.

She carried these feelings into all subsequent interpersonal situations. As defined at the beginning of this chapter, a parataxic distortion is present when an individual deals with another person as if he were someone else, usually a close person from the individual's past. In all interpersonal settings this patient treats other persons as if they were one, or both, of her parents, and she retreats from them.

As often happens in a parataxic distortion, a vicious circle was thus set up. The patient's parataxic distortion prevented her from forming the close relationships which might have had beneficial effects on her. Her parataxic distortion cut her off from interpersonal dealings in which she might gradually have perceived that relationships with people can be gratifying and can build self-esteem.

Her parataxic distortion thus prevented *the tendency toward health* from working in her favor. It obstructed growth toward emotional and interpersonal health. This vicious circle continued until a life crisis at the age of 22 precipitated a florid schizophrenic psychosis.

2. *The Operation of the Parataxic Distortion in the Patient's Day-to-Day Life*

Therapist: You haven't mentioned Dave during the last few sessions. How are you and he getting along?

Patient: I haven't seen him for about a month. He called two or three times. I made a date with him, but I didn't go, and I didn't call. I guess he didn't like that, and he hasn't called since then.

Therapist: Why didn't you go?

Patient: I froze.

Therapist: Froze?

Patient: I guess I got panicky, to use your word. My mother has been pushing him at me. She says he's smart, has a good future and so on, and that I won't find many more boys as good as he is, especially if I keep pushing them away. He was beginning to get interested in me. I can tell when a man is getting interested, often before he can. I know by the way he looks at me, and he begins to talk about what he's going to do in the future, and so forth. Dave is all right, but I just froze. When the time came to meet him, I slipped out of the house and went to a movie, and I didn't come back until about midnight. My mother was furious, and my father didn't like it either.

Therapist: Can you tell me what you felt like when the time for this date approached?

Patient: I guess I got scared. I felt a little sick; I wanted to run, somewhere, anywhere. It was the old feeling we've talked about. I tightened up all over, and all I could think of was to get away.

Therapist: Let's imagine the future together for a minute. What do you think would happen if, by some chance, you and Dave got married?

Patient: I don't like to think about it. But when I do, the first thing I think of is that there aren't many happy marriages. At least, all the ones in our family don't seem happy. My brother's marriage is a mess. He says that if he didn't have two kids he'd get a divorce. If I married Dave it would be the same thing. It almost never works out.

Therapist: Why not?

Patient: The couple get bored with each other. They fight. They use the kids to hurt each other, and the kids are the ones who suffer most in the end.

Therapist: So it's a trap, a trap full of anguish?

Patient: I suppose so. Anyway, that's what it means to me.

Therapist: And so when the time for your date with Dave

approached, you got very tense and fled to the movies. Isn't that pretty much what you did all during your childhood and adolescence to avoid contacts with your parents and other upsetting people?

Patient: I guess so. The mere idea of getting tied up with anybody grinds me, panics me.

Therapist: Would it be fair to say that in fleeing from closeness to people *in your present life* you are acting as if Dave and your parents and other painful people *from your past life* are all wrapped up in one package, and that that package is like a time bomb that will soon go off if you stay around?

Patient: Maybe.

Therapist: And that you, in a sense, are behaving as if Dave were your father, or your mother or some other upsetting person from your past?

Patient: Perhaps. Is there anything we can do about it?

Therapist: If it were hopeless, we wouldn't be here talking about it.

In this abridged dialogue the therapist and the patient have examined how a parataxic distortion which originated in childhood and adolescent experiences distorts the patient's current interpersonal relationships. To use Sullivan's expression, the patient is mistaking Dave for her parents, and perhaps other traumatic persons, in her early life.

3. *The Operation of the Parataxic Distortion in the Patient-Therapist Relationship*

Therapist: You appear to have had trouble finding things to talk about during the last few sessions.

Patient: We seem to be going over the same kinds of things all the time. You must be getting a little bored with this.

Therapist: Do I seem so?

Patient: No, but I guess it's part of your job not to show it. I've been seeing you for over a year now and we've covered just about everything in my life. In general, I'm getting along pretty well now.

Therapist: And so?

Patient: Well, I suppose you'll be wanting to stop pretty soon. You must have people who are sicker than I am.

Therapist: There's still plenty to talk about. Between sessions you have about 50 waking hours, and the majority of that time is spent with people; it can't all go smoothly. Changing the focus a bit, are you feeling a little apprehensive about any aspect of therapy?

Patient: Well, I've been thinking that it may be time for me to begin to go it alone. If therapy goes on and on, I may get hooked on it.

Therapist: Hooked?

Patient: I may begin to lean on it too much; I may become unable to make up my mind about anything or to do anything without first talking it over here.

Therapist: When you say "hooked" on the treatment, do you actually mean that you fear I might get to know too much about you? Does it frighten you that someone might get to know you really well?

Patient: Something like that.

Therapist: And is that dangerous?

Patient: I've made a mess of a lot of things in my life. In time it must get discouraging to you that I still have some problems that aren't completely straightened out.

Therapist: Let your imagination run for a bit. What do you think would happen if I were to get discouraged with you?

Patient: I suppose you'd start making the appointments less frequent, and maybe shorter, and finally you'd stop treatment altogether.

Therapist: In other words, I'd reject you as being a somewhat defective specimen of the human species whom I'd patched up as well as possible for the time being?

Patient: I suppose so.

Therapist: If that were the case, what would be the safe thing for you to do?

Patient: Talk the situation over with you, and agree that we'd gone about as far as we could, and let it go at that.

Therapist: In other words, you'd beat me to the punch. Before I could make a move to get rid of you, you'd take the first step. Would that be less painful for you?

Patient: I guess it would be easier.

Therapist: Is this the same old pattern of fleeing any relationship in which a person may get to know you too well? Does an alarm bell seem to go off and say, "Run, Nancy. If you have too much to do with anyone it begins to hurt, and in time it becomes just plain torture"?

The therapist has here outlined how the patient is carrying her parataxic distortion into the patient-therapist relationship. She is behaving toward the therapist as if he were one or both of her parents. She is repeating with him an old unhealthy pattern from her historic past.

4. *The Functioning of the Tendency Toward Health in Leading the Patient into Sound Patterns of Interpersonal Life When the Obstructing Parataxic Distortion Is Removed*

Patient: Last weekend Larry and I went to a cabin he has at Lake Mitaconga. There was another couple there. At night we made a big fire in the fireplace, made popcorn and drank some special drink Larry learned to make in Mexico last year.

Therapist: Was there anything about the weekend that made you uncomfortable?

Patient: I was a little edgy in the car on the way down, but once we got there I relaxed. From then on everything was fine.

Therapist: No ghosts?

Patient: Ghosts?

Therapist: Shadowy persons from the past standing in corners telling you it's dangerous to get close to people, and that if you do you'll be hurt, and will get caught in a trap and will never get out?

Patient: No ghosts, or at least only a little one who soon went away.

Therapist: Without those ghosts blocking your path you can go forward and discover a new world. How does this world look?

Patient: It looks and feels good. I suppose I'll have my problems, but without ghosts to bother me I ought to be able to solve them.

The therapist has here used a metaphor (ghosts) to indicate that once the patient's parataxic distortions are resolved *the tendency toward health* operates spontaneously to lead her toward healthier patterns of living.

This is, of course, a much simplified case vignette presented in abridged dialogues, and all cases of psychotherapy do not end so satisfactorily. However, it illustrates the handling of parataxic distortions in discussing experiences in the patient's (1) past life, (2) current interpersonal relationships and (3) relationship with the therapist; it also indicates (4) how resolution of parataxic distortions allows *the tendency toward health* to work.

Chapter 8

Special Verbal and Nonverbal Techniques in Psychotherapy

In this chapter we shall discuss seven aspects of Sullivan's treatment techniques that do not fall conveniently in the general categories covered in other chapters.

They are (1) nonverbal communication in psychotherapy (2) the repertory of each therapist, (3) examination of the personified self, (4) the patient's future as an area for exploration, (5) handling transitions in psychotherapy, (6) investigation of abrupt changes in the patient's life adjustment and (7) dreams.

1. NONVERBAL COMMUNICATION IN PSYCHOTHERAPY

Sullivan states that probably more than half of all communication, both in daily life and in psychotherapy, occurs by nonverbal means. He is the only one of the major psychotherapeutic innovators to emphasize the great importance of wordless communication in psychotherapy.

Nonverbal communication in psychotherapy includes the transmission of information by (1) facial expressions, (2) gestures, (3) body movements and body postures, (4) wordless vocal sounds, (5) material objects in the therapist's hands and miscellaneous other ways.

Nonverbal communication occurs from the patient to the therapist and from the therapist to the patient. A therapist should therefore be aware of the data he is transmitting to the patient as well as the data the patient is transmitting to him. Success or failure in treatment often depends on how knowledgeable the therapist is of these things. Sullivan used nonverbal techniques liberally in his own psychotherapy.

In psychotherapy both words and nonverbal methods are, of course, woven together. Each statement or question by both the patient and the therapist is accompanied by vocal intonations as well as a facial expression and a body posture, and frequently by other nonverbal concomitants. There are occasions, however, when nonverbal communication is employed alone.

Some therapists believe that nonverbal communication is eliminated or reduced to a negligible minimum in certain psychotherapeutic situations, such as classical Freudian psychoanalysis in which the therapist sits out of sight of the patient and is silent most of the time. In Chapters 4 and 7 it has been pointed out that actually a great deal of nonverbal communication goes on from the therapist to the patient in this type of treatment, as well as in all other kinds of psychotherapy. Every therapist, therefore, should be aware that no matter what the format of his therapy he is frequently transmitting information nonverbally. He should, therefore, use nonverbal techniques with a certain amount of skill. He is going to employ them whether he wishes or not, and so he might as well use them adeptly.

In the following brief patient-therapist interchanges, various kinds of nonverbal communication occur. In each instance emphasis is put on what the therapist does. However, in every case the patient also is conveying data in wordless ways. Nonverbal techniques will be combined with words in all dialogues for purposes of clarity.

Use of Facial Expressions

Patient: I'm afraid Elaine and Charles could see I was unsure of myself and that I was ruining the whole situation.

Therapist: (*Raises his eyebrows, juts his jaw slightly forward and stares at the patient with a look of skeptical surprise*) And just what did they do to indicate that they thought such depreciating things about you?

Use of Gestures

Patient: I couldn't get up nerve enough to mention sex to her. When I went home I masturbated, and afterward I felt awful; I felt like a puny 13-year-old kid again.

Therapist: (*Spreads his hands before him with his palms upward and with the thumb and fingers fanned apart; he simultaneously makes a slight lateral movement with each hand*) And what's so terrible about that? Sex with her would have been more fun, but was this so shameful?

Use of Body Movements and Body Postures

Patient: I seem to be going over the same things time and time again. You must be getting pretty tired of all this; you're probably thinking it's about time to take a break in treatment or to give it up altogether.

Therapist: (*Leans back in his chair, crosses his right leg over his left knee and lets his arms and hands rest in a relaxed way on the chair arms*) Do I look like I'm getting uptight or bored, and am about to get rid of you?

Use of Wordless Vocal Sounds

Patient: My mother said I was making her sick because of the things I was doing, and my father told me I was the whole cause of her illness.

Therapist: (*Clicks his tongue making the noise usually written tsk! tsk! and then emits a short hmmm!*) Did your parents always throw guilt at you in that way when you did something they didn't like?

Sullivan himself sometimes used a weary sigh, or a stifled groan (which he described as being like the noise made by sand in a set of ball bearings), or a skeptical snort to express disbelief or nonacceptance about some self-deprecatory remark or glaring rationalization a patient made. A therapist often can render a patient much service by indicating through such wordless vocal sounds that he does not consider what the patient has just said to be awful, or shocking, or shameful or loathsome.

Use of Material Objects

Patient: I've been thinking a lot about Debbie lately. It seems that when she and I broke up . . . (continues talking). . . .
Therapist: (*Snuffs out a cigarette, picks up a clipboard and jots a few notes*)

The therapist has used material objects (cigarette, clipboard and ballpoint pen) to say, "This is relevant, interesting material. Go on." He may or may not have been aware of saying this nonverbally, and it may or may not have been desirable to convey this message.

This survey does not exhaust the range of nonverbal communicative techniques; it merely covers some of the main ones.

Vocal intonations fall in a special category of their own, halfway between verbal and nonverbal methods. For example, depending on vocal intonations, "No" as a single word response to a question can say quite different things. If a patient asks whether something represents a setback in his therapy, the therapist may say "No" in a flat, noncommittal way that puzzles the patient, or in an emphatic manner that reassures him, or in a hesitant tone that frightens him, or in a questioning way that invites him to talk, or in a curt way that shuts the subject off, or in an amused way that makes the patient feel that he asked a silly question. A therapist knows what he is communicating only if he is aware of the nonverbal information he transmits in each utterance and act.

As noted above, the therapist also should be constantly alert to what the patient is saying nonverbally. Anxiousness may be betrayed by subtle changes of posture and minor alterations of voice pitch. Irritability may be indicated by tensing of facial musculature and a slight narrowing of the eyes. The variety of information that patients convey nonverbally is great, and the therapist who is attentive to it is much more aware of what is going on.

2. THE REPERTORY OF EACH THERAPIST

Recognizing that psychotherapy is an individualized craft, Sullivan states that each therapist builds a repertory of therapeutic techniques that work best for him. From the wide spectrum of available verbal and nonverbal methods, each therapist in time selects the ones he handles most effectively, and these constitute his treatment repertory.

During the first several years of his work, a psychotherapist as a rule should stick to standard techniques, such as those outlined in previous chapters of this book. After that he can begin to add to his repertory things that function well for him but may not be useful for many other therapists.

A case in point is the use of melodrama in therapy. Sullivan himself was adept in employing melodramatic techniques; he utilized skillfully methods that in the hands of many other therapists would miscarry. On one occasion, for example,

Sullivan was consulted by a frightened patient who was much in awe of the well-known therapist to whom he had been referred. Sensing this, Sullivan spent the first several minutes of the initial session searching the drawers and the top of his desk for an allegedly missing paper, while muttering, "Where did I put that thing? Where on earth can it be?" By the time Sullivan finished this apparent search, the patient had lost his awe and could begin to talk easily about his problems.

Sullivan often employed such histrionic maneuvers to make points forcefully. For example, if a patient told him that his relationships with his parents and his marital partner were wonderful and had always been so, and that he had never had even minor difficulties with these persons, Sullivan might register his skepticism by removing his glasses, staring at the patient in astonishment and exclaiming, "Extraordinary!"

In a similar vein, Sullivan feels that some therapists can employ signs of mild boredom, or amusement, or irritation to make a point or convey an attitude. For example, if a patient talks at length about the interpersonal staleness and triviality of his relationships with his parents, or friends or others, the therapist may assume an appearance of fatigue and say with a sigh, "All this must get rather tiresome at times. Do you sometimes yearn for more vibrant relationships with people?" If a patient relates an episode in which his marital partner or some other close person caused an uproar over some inconsequential point, and the therapist wishes to lessen the patient's tension about it, he may say, "Who needs television with things like this going on at home?" If a patient recounts an episode in which he was callously exploited by someone, the therapist may frown and say with slight vexation, "Do you often allow people to get away with things like that?" Such melodramatic procedures should be brief and emphatic; they should not be repetitious and should be utilized sparingly and only by therapists who can handle them well. Moreover, the boredom, or amusement, or irritation or other melodramatic feeling is never directed *at the patient*, but at the thing, or situation, or person whom he and the therapist are discussing.

After employing a special operation, such as a melodramatic procedure, the therapist as a rule should go on to deal with the broader issue of which the specific incident is an example. "Well, this indicates that the sooner you can settle this problem with them, the sooner you will be free of this kind of exploitation, and that will be healthier for everyone concerned." "I suppose this sort of thing has happened before, perhaps many times. Can you tell me about other such incidents?" "This was an upsetting experience, but let's try to get something out of it."

Humor is a difficult thing to employ in therapy, and it should be used only by the minority of therapists who can handle it skillfully. The main dangers are that the patient may feel that the therapist is taking his problems lightly, or is directing the witticisms *at him*. However, in adept hands humor sometimes can be utilized to break tension or to put something into a broader perspective. As an example of the latter case, a therapist may inquire, "Did your father think he was King Kong, or maybe Super-Daddy?" to deflate a bullying, awesome father to a smaller size so the patient can discuss him more comfortably. Timing is crucial in humor, and it rarely achieves its tension-reducing effect unless it is spontaneous; premeditated humor usually falls flat and makes the patient uncomfortable.

Sarcasm and irony miscarry frequently in therapy. Sullivan, however, used them effectively at times. For example, to indicate that something the patient said was not as frightening as the patient felt, Sullivan might say, "Goodness! Such things ought to send shivers up my spine." The voice inflections and facial expressions that accompany such comments usually determine whether they succeed or fail. Unless a therapist is sure of his ability to handle these techniques and knows his patient well enough to judge their effect, he is best advised not to employ them.

As a rule successful therapy requires that the cultures and language usages of the patient and the therapist dovetail fairly well. When they do not, the patient and the therapist may be using words and expressions in quite different ways, and one or both of them may be unaware of it; also, their concepts of acceptable social conduct may not coincide. Sullivan feels that these problems are more common than many therapists realize. To cite a current example, a therapist who comes from a suburban, professional class background may not grasp the meanings of many words and expressions in the argot of an inner city, ghetto black adolescent. In another case a therapist from a sophisticated, sexually permissive background may not comprehend the strict rules about the sexual behavior of an adolescent girl that prevail in a Puerto Rican family that has recently come to a large metropolitan area from a rural island background. A therapist should at least be aware that such problems exist, and he often must work hard to widen his perspectives and adapt them to the linguistic customs and social conditions of his patient. If such obstacles are great and the therapist cannot make progress on them, it may be advisable to refer the patient to a therapist who better understands the culture and language of the patient.

Every therapist should, moreover, recognize that he has gaps in his experience in living that may cause difficulties with some patients. To cite a simple example, a therapist who was reared in economically difficult circumstances may find it hard to comprehend the distress of a wealthy patient about articles the patient feels are necessities and the therapist views as frivolous luxuries. A heterosexual therapist often must work hard to envision the familial and social dilemmas of a homosexual. A therapist from an agnostic or nonbelieving background may find it difficult to grasp the anguish that lifelong religious fundamentalists feel about various problems of conduct and belief. Though some therapists can bridge these gaps easily, others have problems in doing so. Awareness of such situations and frank admissions of them are sometimes advisable; an approach which says, in essence, "Let's try to understand this together" is often useful.

Sullivan feels that candid recognition of cultural differences, coupled with sincere efforts to reach the patient, offer the therapist a chance to grow; it widens his experience about the manifold kinds of interpersonal life in the society in which he lives. It also emphasizes to both the patient and the therapist that the therapist is not an omniscient deity but simply another human being who has extensive, but never complete, expertise in helping people who have troubles in living.

3. EXAMINATION OF THE PERSONIFIED SELF

Sullivan uses the term *personified self* to designate *all the things a person can describe about himself*. It denotes more or less the same thing that often is called the self-image, or the conscious self-image.

Examination of the personified self is sometimes a useful psychotherapeutic technique. In some cases it may be employed systematically; for example, the therapist may say, "Perhaps it would be useful for us to discuss in some detail how you see yourself and your relationships with other people." In other cases it may be considered in fragments, with evaluation of various facets of it from time to time during a course of psychotherapy.

In examining the personified self, the therapist is always concerned with the soundness of the patient's ideas about himself. How accurately does he see himself and his relationships with people? In this connection, what things about himself does the patient esteem and what things does he censure? If a patient states that he values his capacity to withstand interpersonal stress and censures his occasional weaknesses in letting other people upset him, what does he mean? By his "capacity to withstand interpersonal stress" he may really be referring to an aloof indifference to the emotional needs and suffering of others; when close people around him become upset, he is coldly indifferent to it. On the other hand he may mean that when important people about him become distraught he retires into a seclusive shell and considers it a weakness if they upset him also. However, the patient may in fact mean that he has, or feels he has, much inner emotional calm and secure self-esteem that enable him to cope with interpersonal stress in an anxiety-free, effective manner. In evaluating a person's personified self, the therapist and the patient explore how he sees himself and what he means by what he says about himself.

When people describe themselves, they often use clichés which they have employed for decades to disguise from themselves and others their true feelings and interpersonal patterns. A great deal of valuable psychotherapeutic work may be done by getting behind these hackneyed expressions and discovering what really goes on in the patient's life.

Investigation of the kinds of interpersonal situations which the patient says make him anxious is often another useful aspect of a survey of the personified self. In what types of settings is he comfortable, and what kinds of relationships reassure him? An inventory of this type can cover such diverse activities as social closeness to individuals of the opposite sex, genital intimacies, resistance to the impositions of a work colleague, demanding a refund for defective merchandise at a store, and a wide range of other major and minor interpersonal activities.

How worthwhile does a person feel he is? How does he rate himself in comparison with other people in terms of social skills, intellectual capacities, likability, vocational abilities and many other things? Does he feel shame and guilt about various things he does, or has done, and what are these things that make him feel ashamed and guilty? To what sorts of interpersonal relationships are they linked? How easily can warped views about himself be corrected? An entire course of psychotherapy could be built on a comprehensive survey and investigation of a patient's personified self.

Does a person have a sense of humor, and what are its characteristics? Sullivan defines a sense of humor as a person's capacity for seeing in an anxiety-free way his true significance in the various interpersonal situations in which he lives. Many people might argue about this definition of the elusive thing called a sense of humor, but there probably is a good deal of truth in it; Sullivan characteristically puts his definition in interpersonal terms. Humor thus becomes linked to the values a person puts on the things in his life and to how he views his own roles in diverse situations. In evaluating a patient's sense of humor, a therapist should ask, among other things, "Can you laugh at things which show up some of your own mistakes and limitations?" "If you can't occasionally laugh at yourself, do you have any ideas why not?" "Does frank recognition of your shortcomings upset you in some way?"

Systematic inquiry into the patient's personified self (self-image, or conscious self-image) may be particularly useful with patients who have trouble getting started in psychotherapy. It also can be serviceable when therapy becomes stalemated and the patient has difficulty finding new things to discuss.

4. THE PATIENT'S FUTURE AS AN AREA FOR EXPLORATION

It is sometimes useful in therapy to examine the patient's speculations about his future. Where are his interpersonal relationships leading him? If things continue as they are now, what will the patient's life be like three years, or five years or ten years in the future?

The object of such inquiries is to cast new light on the present and to some extent on the past. The patient's current life patterns often become more meaningful and are seen in new ways if they are examined in terms of future possibilities. Sullivan is, so far as I know, the only distinguished psychiatric innovator who emphasizes the patient's future as a fruitful area for investigation.

In approaching this subject, the therapist, for instance, may say, "Sometimes it is useful for a person to take a look at where he may be going. Let your imagination run free. Based on what is occurring now in your marriage [or whatever area of the patient's life is under consideration], and on what has happened in recent months and years, what do you feel your relationship with your marital partner will be five years from now?"

The therapist may go on to ask, in essence, "What does this tell you about the things that are going on now?" "What can be done to avoid the undesirable things you see as future possibilities?" "What could be done to encourage the healthier things which you see as alternate possibilities?" "Can you in any way mobilize people around you, or rearrange your life, to work toward a sounder future?"

The therapist must be careful not to allow examinations of the future to arouse undue levels of anxiety in the patient; he should not permit them to demoralize the patient and to precipitate depressiveness and feelings of hopelessness. The therapist's theme should be, "We are merely looking at *possibilities* concerning the future, and our purpose is to plan action to prevent unhealthy things from occurring. If the outlook seems bleak, we are learning something which will help you to build another kind of future for yourself. The time to begin to solve these difficulties is now, not five years from now when they are already upon you."

Sullivan acknowledges that investigation of elaborate fantasies of having great wealth, political prominence, fame and other things reveals something about a person. However, he does not encourage introspective, detailed exploration of such fantasies. He feels that examination of the patient's forward looking speculations about more realistic things in his life is a much more fruitful kind of therapeutic activity.

5. HANDLING TRANSITIONS IN PSYCHOTHERAPY

Making a transition from one subject to another in an interview sometimes poses problems. How does the therapist shift the focus of an interview from one area of the patient's life to another without jolting him or seeming to dismiss the previous topic in a brusque, insensitive manner?

Sullivan dedicates much attention to this subject. He divides transitions into (1) *smooth transitions*, (2) *accentuated transitions* and (3) *abrupt transitions*. The first two types of transitions are frequently used; the third is employed only in exceptional conditions.

Smooth Transitions

In a smooth transition the direction of the interview is changed subtly. The transition is a reasonable step in exploring the area of the patient's life that is under discussion. "That leads us into considering such and such." "It would seem that this takes us into examining how you and your parents dealt with this kind of difficulty." "That type of upset often is caused by friction between people; were you by any chance in conflict with anyone at that time?" Smooth transitions are the most common ones employed in well conducted therapy, and the most desirable.

Accentuated Transitions

In an accentuated transition a marked change of focus occurs, or the interview shifts into a new area that is only peripherally related to the previous one.

The patient should be prepared for such a change, and this is best done by nonverbal methods which alert him to the approaching shift of attention. The therapist may make an audible throat clearing noise, and this may be accompanied by an alteration of body posture. The therapist, for example, may uncross his legs, put both feet on the floor and incline his body forward in his chair. In another instance, he may remove his hands from the arms of his chair and clasp them together in front of him while moving his head and body slightly toward the patient; he may turn his gaze from a point which is about 90 degrees on the right or left of the patient to the patient's face. Each therapist employs the postural changes, gestures, facial expressions and other nonverbal operations that are most natural for him. An accentuated transition is deliberate, but the nonverbal steps which play a large part in preparing the patient for it should be as spontaneous as possible.

As he makes an accentuated transition, the therapist should not appear to shut the previous topic off permanently nor to belittle its importance. He simply indicates that a new direction is being taken. "These things are important, but let's turn our attention for a while to such and such." "This undoubtedly had a considerable emotional impact on you, but let's look now at a different facet of your life." "Leaving this subject for a while, do you sometimes feel that. . . ?"

Abrupt Transitions

Abrupt transitions are the least employed of the three types. They are used only when the first two types are not practical, or when a change is urgently needed. An abrupt transition may, for instance, be utilized to shift attention away from a topic about which the patient is becoming so upset that the continuance of the interview is threatened. As a patient becomes panicky and begins to balk, the therapist may say, "You're becoming tense about this, aren't you? Well, we have plenty of time ahead of us. We can let it go for the time being and turn our attention to such and such, can't we?" In another case the therapist may make an abrupt transition by saying, "This is a pretty difficult thing to talk about, isn't it? Well, there's no need to go into it now. Let's go back to considering your relationship with. . . ."

An experienced therapist who knows his patient well may on infrequent occasions use an abrupt transition to precipitate anxiety and thus bring an important subject into sharp focus. However, a therapist should do this only when he can see his path clearly through an anxiety-filled stretch of interview to a comfortable goal beyond, and the goal should be reached by the end of the same interview. The therapist should not leave his patient in turmoil at the termination of the interview. When a therapist has doubts about using an abrupt transition of this kind, he should not employ it.

Some examples of anxiety-precipitating abrupt transitions follow. "Turning our attention to a different topic, do you sometimes feel a certain amount of homosexual arousal when you are with him?" "Let's consider another facet of this. Do you feel that at times the hostility within you threatens to lead you into open violence?" "Returning to something we barely touched on a couple of interviews back, does it seem at times that your hold on reality is slipping away from you and that there is nothing you can do about it?" A therapist employs anxiety arousing abrupt transitions only when he is sure he can help the patient to achieve some important insight, and to regain a sound level of emotional comfort by the time the session ends.

6. INVESTIGATION OF ABRUPT CHANGES IN THE PATIENT'S LIFE ADJUSTMENT

Abrupt changes in patients' life adjustments often are fruitful areas for exploration. Thus, if a patient's life was going well until about eight months previously, and a sudden interpersonal and emotional deterioration occurred, examination of *how* and *why* it happened may be revealing and important.

A patient often has difficulty describing how his life altered at some critical point. He tends to fall back on trite statements, such as "I didn't feel like going out much," "I lost interest in people, that's all," or "Things went stale in our marriage." Such statements do not really describe *how* the patient's life changed; they merely indicate that a change occurred. Sullivan stresses that a therapist should never "let a patient get away with a statement like this." Behind it often lies a great deal of important data.

For example, if a patient says, "I lost interest in school about then," the therapist first wants to know when "about then" was. He and the patient next explore exactly what the patient did when he "lost interest in school." Did he continue to perform adequately in school despite boredom and apathy? Did he begin to miss classes? Did he fail to complete papers and other projects? Did he skip seminars and examinations? The therapist next investigates what the general level of the patient's school performance was *before* this change happened. Was he frequently negligent in any or all of these activities during his first three semesters in college? Did he have difficulties of this sort in high school? The therapist must ascertain not only that a change occurred at a particular time, but also how marked the change was.

What were the interpersonal consequences of this change? Did his teachers, or anyone else, inquire what the trouble was? What were the reactions of his roommate, his friends, his parents and others? How did the patient explain this change to people, and what did they reply? In this inquiry the therapist is as attentive to all the things that *did not happen* as to those that did. For instance, if no one commented on this change, *why* didn't they do so?

What did the patient anticipate would be the consequences of abandoning his school work, and how did he plan to handle those consequences? Did he plan to go to work, or to join a commune or to take up some new life style, and with whom did he discuss these things? There are always many incidental by-products of this kind of exploration; the patient, for example, may for the first time begin to see how practical or impractical his plans were.

One or more interviews could in this manner be devoted to scrutinizing exactly *what occurred* when this change in the patient's life took place. Until this point the therapist and the patient have mainly discussed factual details. Except in superficial ways, they have not examined what was going on *emotionally* and *interpersonally*. They have been talking about *how* the change occurred, but not *why*. They next turn their attention to this area.

Was the patient embroiled in a turbulent relationship with one or both of his parents when this change occurred and, if so, what was the nature of his conflict with them? Was he rebelling, or was he for the first time coming to grips with their lack of interest in him, or was he upset about their impending divorce? Was he having difficulties with a girl friend or with a close friend of his own sex, and what were the details of this situation? In short, the therapist and the patient examine in detail what was going on *interpersonally* and *emotionally* in the patient's life when this alteration took place. This leads into evaluation of the *past history* of any relevant interpersonal difficulties. How did his difficulties with his parents or with other persons develop? Such problems often are the products of long chains of interpersonal events, and the material for investigation may be extensive.

In clinical practice, of course, a psychotherapeutic exploration rarely proceeds as methodically as this outline suggests; the patient and the therapist crisscross and backtrack through wide ranges of material as the interviews proceed. Also, much emphasis is placed on how the patient and the people around him *felt* about the events and relationships in which they were participating. How did the patient feel at the time about this change in his life? How does he feel about it now? What feelings are noteworthy because he *did* not have them, and perhaps does not have them now?

In some instances an investigation of an abrupt change in a patient's life adjustment develops into a lengthy process, and a course of psychotherapy with specific or limited goals might consist almost entirely of such an exploration.

7. DREAMS

It should be stated at the outset that Sullivan's views on the use of dreams in psychotherapy are markedly different from those of Freud. Sullivan's criticisms of Freudian dream analysis were during his life one of various causes of friction between him and Freud's adherents, and have contributed to their continued rejection of Sullivan's concepts since his death in 1949.

Sullivan feels that it is never possible to discuss the true content of a dream with any degree of accuracy. In addition to problems in remembering a dream, the patient always distorts its narrative greatly in telling it. His anxieties cause him to omit many details, to add things that were not in the dream and to change many other features of it. Sullivan is not here referring to the Freudian concept that the latent content of a dream is much contorted by symbolisms in producing its manifest content. Sullivan feels that a dream strikes too near a patient's naked emotional problems, and the patient therefore grossly deforms the manifest content of the dream in telling it; hence the dream narrative which he relates to the therapist is not what he dreamed. As a result, the actual dream is never available for reliable discussion. It is therefore impossible to "analyze" a dream.

Sullivan feels, moreover, that there is no scientifically valid way to determine whether an interpretation of any part of a dream is correct or incorrect. For example, using a simplified case for ease in presentation, a patient *states* that he dreamed a rabbit was being attacked by a wolf; after extensive discussion of the dream, probably using free associative techniques, the therapist says that the rabbit represents the patient, the wolf represents his father, and the dream's basic theme is the patient's feelings of fearfulness toward his father. How can *scientific* evidence be assembled which will demonstrate to any reasonably well trained observer that this interpretation is correct? How can repeatable, predictable *scientific* experiments be set up to prove or disprove this interpretation of the dream? Sullivan feels no method for doing this exists, and he doubts any method will ever be discovered. Sullivan is, of course, rejecting Freud's method of free association; he does not consider it valid since there is no way of proving that conclusions reached by it are accurate. He feels Freud never demonstrated, or felt it necessary to demonstrate, the validity of free association in objective scientific ways. Freud merely assumed it was valid; this is one of the basic *assumptions* on which he built psychoanalysis.

A fundamental aspect of this problem is that a dream is a purely mental phenomenon. It is not an *interpersonal* experience since only one person, the dreamer, is involved. This point is made clear in the following contrasting examples. If a child is beaten by his father while his mother protests, three people are involved in this *interpersonal* event; data can be gathered from all three of them to determine what actually happened and how they felt about it. However, if a person dreams that a rabbit is attacked by a wolf, a purely mental phenomenon occurs. The dreamer is the only source of information about it and he is in a state of greatly decreased observational capacity by virtue of being asleep.

A dream is, in addition, a *nonsensory* experience. A person does not see, hear or touch anything in a dream; this makes remembering it difficult and *proving* anything about its content impossible from the viewpoint of strict scientific *logic*. Any reader who is interested in going further into this knotty problem should consult the works of the distinguished Austrian-British philosopher of science, Sir Karl Popper, who in recent decades has dealt extensively with the scientific problems of Freudian psychoanalysis. In Britain, and gradually in other areas of the world, Popper is coming to be regarded as the most important authority on the logic and philosophy of science since Francis Bacon. Sullivan and Popper did not influence each other; they developed independently, but their ideas dovetail remarkably well on psychiatric subjects.

Sullivan feels, however, that dreams can be used in psychotherapy if these limitations are recognized. A dream *is* an experience, and a patient can discuss it in the same sense that he can talk about any other experience he had. The patient can relate his *reminiscence* of the dream and the feelings the *reminiscence* arouses in him. He can discuss what it means to him and can talk about the emotional and intellectual impact it had on him; he can examine the feelings of horror, or sexual arousal, or loneliness, or desperation which he feels in recounting the dream, or which he had on awakening from it.

However, Sullivan feels that a useful discussion of a dream *must lead to exploration of interpersonal events and relationships in the patient's waking life.* Thus, after the patient gives his reminiscence of the dream and the feelings aroused in recounting it, the therapist may ask, "Have you ever felt this way in any daytime experience in your life?" "What kinds of experiences between you and other people does this dream suggest?" "What does this dream mean to you in terms of your relationships with people in present and past situations?"

The dream thus serves as the starting point for discussing some area of the patient's life. As such, dreams can be useful with some patients. Sullivan emphasizes, however, that this is a far cry from "analyzing the content" of a dream.

The following abridged dialogue illustrates such use of dreams in psychotherapy. In it the patient has just finished recounting his reminiscence of a dream in which a small, defenseless animal was attacked by a vicious predator.

Therapist: As you think about this dream, what feelings do you have?

Patient: I feel uneasy, almost a little fearful. It's more than just squeamishness. I don't like to think about it.

Therapist: Does this suggest anything in your current or past life experiences?

Patient: I usually feel a certain edginess when I'm around people who have any authority over me, any kind of power. I've always been a little ill at ease with teachers, and with bosses on jobs and with other people like that. It's a sort of "What will they do to me?" feeling.

Therapist: Do you mean, what *harmful* things may they do to you?

Patient: I guess so. It's a feeling that in some way I'm helpless, maybe somewhat defenseless, against anyone who has authority or power over any aspect of my life.

Therapist: Can you give me a specific example of this in your relationship with some person?

Here the patient and the therapist have taken the remembered dream narrative and its associated feelings as bases for launching into an exploration of an area of the patient's interpersonal experience. This process could continue during a number of interviews and could deal with experiences from early childhood onward. Sullivan feels that this is the only legitimate use of dreams. He feels, moreover, that examination of dreams in psychotherapy is optional; in many cases they are not utilized. Discussion of dreams may be of value if therapy bogs down and the patient can find little to talk about. They also tend to be more useful with patients who have a somewhat sophisticated understanding of the nature and goals of psychotherapy.

Chapter 9

Methods for Dealing with Various Kinds of Psychotherapeutic Problems

In this chapter we shall consider methods for dealing with five categories of problems encountered in psychotherapy. We shall discuss these categories under the following headings: (1) management of deteriorating communication, (2) harmful topics, (3) handling jargon, (4) the principle of reciprocal emotions and its relation to therapeutic difficulties and (5) special problems in modified, or brief, psychotherapy.

1. THE MANAGEMENT OF DETERIORATING COMMUNICATION

When communication between the patient and the therapist deteriorates, and interviews become unproductive or stagnate in long periods of silence, the therapist should evaluate what is going on, or has gone on, to produce this situation.

We shall review some of the things which may contribute to it.

Mobilization of Undue Anxiety in the Patient

A therapist sometimes probes a painful area too bluntly or quickly and arouses so much emotional distress in the patient that he becomes evasive, or silent or able to talk only about trivia. The therapist may be unaware that his questions or comments were so upsetting; he knows only that communication between the patient and him has worsened.

Patient: After a couple of years of marriage, Susan and I began to argue a lot and drift apart. We couldn't agree on anything. Finally, we broke up.

Therapist: In these arguments did she often bring up your occasional impotence?

Patient: No, not very often; it wasn't much of a problem at that time. Our first big argument was over the car. She wanted to trade in our Belcampo station wagon and buy a Chelsea, but I . . . (talks at length about the details of their arguments over a car trade-in). . . .

In this condensed interchange the therapist probed insensitively into a painful area (the patient's problem with sexual impotence) and mobilized so much anxiety that the patient digressed into an irrelevant subject. Depending on circumstances, such a digression may last from a few minutes to a few interviews. Frequent repetition of this error may produce persistent deterioration of communication.

Avoidance of such mistakes requires continual attentiveness by the therapist, since it often is hard to predict what will arouse undue levels of anxiety in a patient. The clues which alert a therapist to an upsurge of anxiety in many instances are nonverbal. Emotional distress frequently is betrayed by tenseness of facial muscles, body restlessness, gripping of chair arms, and other wordless acts. A lapse into silence or a deviation into talkativeness on insignificant topics may indicate that an emotional sore spot has been too roughly touched. Changes of vocal intonation often signal anxiety. Constant vigilance is necessary to detect rising anxiety and to prevent it from obstructing therapy. Much of Chapter 3 is devoted to the subject of anxiety as an impeding force in psychotherapy; it complements this present discussion.

When the therapist feels that he perhaps has contributed to the stagnation of therapy by precipitating a high measure of anxiety, he may inquire if he has done anything to upset the patient. "I wonder if I've said or done anything that has made you tense and less able to talk freely. Can you put your finger on anything that has upset you?" In many instances, however, it is better to treat the difficulty as an error in the patient-therapist collaboration rather than owing to anything done by either the therapist or the patient. For example, the therapist may say, "I feel that somewhere we took a wrong turn a while back and have gotten into territory that's pretty uncomfortable for you. As a result, we've had difficulty talking lately."

In some cases the therapist can individually review the recent course of therapy and can determine what mobilizes anxiety in the patient. In other instances he may wish to do this in collaboration with a colleague or a psychotherapeutic supervisor.

The Therapist Should Review His Former Opinion That Things Were Going Well in Therapy

When communication is poor, the therapist should take a backward look to see if his former impression of good communication was justified. In retrospect, the therapist may find that the patient talked fluently but skirted all major problems. He may realize that while the patient seemed to accept his comments he was not allowing them to affect his modes of feeling and thinking. Poor communication may for appreciable periods of time be camouflaged by the patient's glibness and anxiousness to make a favorable impression on the therapist by being "a good patient." A certain amount of psychiatric jargon is used in this process, and the patient goes through the motions of therapy without true emotional involvement in it.

The therapist can in these cases examine the present and past state of therapy by asking himself some pointed questions. Have the patient and I really identified some significant problems in his life, and have we been working on them? Have we actually discovered the things that brought him to therapy? Is he coming to therapy because he feels a need for it, or because of pressure from his marital partner, his parents, his employers or others? Did this patient have a fairly clear concept of what was involved in treatment when he began it, and was this the kind of experience he was seeking?

The Therapist Should Identify Any Discouraging Things the Patient Has Experienced in the Treatment Sessions

Sullivan feels that a therapist should do nothing during therapeutic sessions to demoralize the patient. Words and actions which lead the patient to feel hopeless about his difficulties should be avoided. A therapist may perceive discouraging limitations to what can be accomplished in therapy, but he should be cautious about discussing these limitations in disheartening ways.

Patient: In addition to these other problems, I have a lot of tension in my job.

Therapist: That is an area of your life we cannot change. We should concentrate on things we may be able to alter.

The therapist in this brief interchange may be correct, but he probably has discouraged the patient about a segment of his life which is important to him. Several discouraging statements of this kind may lead to a general deterioration of communication. In this case the therapist would have done better to have remained silent on the subject; he perhaps should have directed the dialogue into another region of the patient's experience by means of a leading question, or should have allowed the patient to talk to some extent about his difficulties in his job situation despite his feeling that he could offer the patient little help in this area.

This does not mean that the therapist is a cheerful optimist about everything or that he distributes encouragement indiscriminately. It means only that he avoids saying things that demoralize the patient and cause therapeutic communication to deteriorate. In many cases the more disheartening areas of the patient's life may be approached at a later stage in therapy when the patient has acquired emotional strengths and interpersonal flexibilities that enable him to deal more effectively with grim features of his life situation.

The Therapist Should Evaluate Whether Deterioration in Communication Is Owing to a Change in His Own Attitude Toward the Patient

When communication stagnates, the therapist in many cases should ask himself whether the patient has said and done things which have irritated him, or have made him anxious or have in some other way upset him. As a result, has the therapist's attitude toward the patient changed, and is this an important contributant to deteriorated communication?

Many patients quickly sense alterations in therapists' attitudes toward them, though often they are not articulately aware of the changes and cannot describe them. As a result their spontaneity and comfortable involvement in therapy decrease. The patient often perceives a change in the therapist's attitude by his facial expressions, body movements, voice intonations, and other nonverbal acts which convey boredom, irritability, discouragement about the patient, anxiousness, or other feelings which dampen therapy. The patient may detect such changes long before the therapist becomes aware of them.

We are not here discussing reactions of therapists which in psychoanalysis are termed counter-transference; counter-transference consists of feelings of the therapist toward the patient which, at least in part, are produced by the therapist's own past history and personality difficulties. We are here considering a therapist's attitudes which arise in the context of the ongoing, give-and-take interpersonal relationship between him and the patient, and we are assuming that the therapist is a reasonably well-adjusted person.

Every therapist has, whether he is aware of it or not, an attitude toward each of his patients. This is inescapable; therapists are human beings and not machines. The important thing is that the therapist be alertly aware of his attitude as he carries out his role of a *participant observer* in the therapeutic process. The therapist always should be *observing himself* as well as the patient. There are many common illustrations of this. For example, therapists as a rule tend to like patients who talk easily and make good progress in solving their problems. These patients confirm the therapist's view of himself as a skillful, helpful professional person. Many therapists tend to feel less positively toward patients who do not talk well and seem to be getting little out of treatment. These patients tend to erode the therapist's concept of himself as an able, useful professional worker. Many other examples of this kind could be cited.

A therapist who keeps in mind his role as a *participant observer* in the therapeutic process notes his reactions, learns something from them and does not allow them to cloud his view of the patient. He does not rationalize his irritable or discouraged feelings, and excuse his failure to help the patient by saying, "The patient would not cooperate in the treatment process." "The patient has a psychotic core that was not apparent earlier in treatment." "Better screening would have shown that this patient is not a good candidate for psychotherapy." Instead, the therapist frankly notes the frustration, discouragement or impatience the patient arouses in him, and he does not allow these feelings to cause therapeutic communication to deteriorate.

When communication degenerates, the therapist in many instances may discuss it candidly with the patient. "During recent sessions I have had the feeling that we are not working together as well as previously. Do you feel the same way?" The therapist may add, "I wonder if I have done or said anything that has made you anxious, or discouraged or perturbed in any way?" In appropriate cases the therapist may simply note the deteriorating communication and ask, "Can you put your finger on what is bothering you?"

It obviously is better, whenever possible, to prevent deterioration of communication than to deal with it when it is full-blown. Most of the material of this book, and especially in the first five chapters, is concerned with many aspects of maintaining the patient-therapist dialogue on a vibrant, productive level.

In occasional cases of deteriorated communication Sullivan advises the use of *free verbalization*. Though free verbalization has a superficial resemblance to Freudian free association, its uses and purposes are quite different. A therapist employing Freudian free association as a rule employs it as the main method of therapy over a period of months or years, whereas Sullivan views free verbalization merely as a tool for occasional use in alleviating deteriorated communication. The therapist applying free association feels that by it he is uncovering unconscious conflicts and feelings that otherwise would be unreachable, whereas Sullivan is skeptical that this actually occurs.

Instead, he recommends that when therapy has stagnated new vigor sometimes can be infused into it if the therapist says, "Tell me as fully as possible the things that come to mind as you think about this aspect of your life." The therapist uses free verbalization as a lubricating agent to get the wheels of therapy moving again; he sees it as no more than that. Moreover, the utility of free verbalization varies much from one patient to another. Many patients find it a difficult or impossible task; their anxiety prevents such uninhibited exposition of their feelings, thoughts and urges. It is most likely to be useful with well educated patients who have a fairly sophisticated understanding of psychotherapy.

2. HARMFUL TOPICS

Sullivan feels that extensive exploration of the patient's fantasy life, especially in its more elaborate and unrealistic spheres, is unlikely to help him. The patient's past and present interpersonal life is a more profitable, and less dangerous, area for investigation.

A patient's deeply concealed, complex fantasy life may be interesting, and often it is quite revealing about many features of the patient's psychology, but Sullivan believes that delving into it is not therapeutically useful and frequently is quite disturbing. He feels that if a patient begins to talk at length about this area the therapist should intervene and say, in essence, "These things tell us something about your inner life, but we shall use our time more effectively if we talk about your past and present relationships with people, and what they mean to you. For example, let's take a closer look at what went on between you and your parents when you. . . ." Sullivan's viewpoints on this subject obviously differ from those of psychoanalysis, which puts emphasis on examination of the patient's fantasy life.

Though he never cites it, Sullivan clearly believes in the first rule of Hippocrates, "First of all, do no harm." He repeatedly stresses that a therapist should hesitate to elicit information that is more likely to upset than to aid a patient. He feels, for example, that premature investigation of a patient's sex life is a common error in psychotherapy, and that early, blunt probing of a patient's painful relationships with his parents is another. Sullivan's main question is not, "Is this material revealing?" but, "Is this material *therapeutically useful?*"

Investigation of an area that severely undermines a patient's feelings of self-esteem and value as a person should be carried out with extreme caution. If it proves too disturbing to the patient, the therapist should desist from this line of inquiry, though he frequently holds open the possibility, at least in his own thinking, that this subject may be approached again later in therapy when the patient is emotionally more secure.

A therapist should not allow a patient to begin discussion of a severely disturbing event unless there is enough time left in the interview to permit an adequate evaluation of it; the patient should not be cut off in the midst of discussing a particularly upsetting incident. For example, if near the end of an interview a patient begins to talk about an anxiety-ridden sexual experience, the therapist may feel it wise to indicate that the topic merits more careful consideration than the short remaining time will allow.

Sullivan himself was at times more flexible than most therapists about the amount of time he spent in an interview. He sometimes allowed a session to go on for up to an hour and a half or even two hours if he felt the patient had intense urgency to talk about a subject. He did this particularly if he felt the patient might never return to the subject if prematurely stopped or if the interview were ended before some of the patient's anxiety on the matter had been decreased to a more comfortable level.

There is a subtle difference of viewpoint between the flexibility Sullivan exercised in psychotherapy and the set unit-of-time concept that commonly prevails in psychotherapeutic work. Most of the persons who pioneered psychotherapy in the first part of this century "leased time" to patients. For a set fee the patient was given regular periods of time each week, usually in units of 50 minutes each, to work on his problems. Sullivan, on the other hand, feels that the therapist is primarily giving *an interpersonal service* in which the units of time must occasionally be molded to meet the patient's needs.

Many therapists today find it impractical to work as Sullivan recommends; they work with full schedules and cannot let any session go much beyond its allotted time without throwing the day's schedule into disarray. Hence, when confronted with a problem of this sort, most therapists must, in essence, say, "This is an emotionally charged, important topic. However, we have little time left today, and if we begin to discuss it we shall have to stop before we have a chance to give it the attention it requires. To begin to talk about this subject and to break off in the middle might be upsetting to you. Perhaps we should hold it over until next time. I hope it will not seem that I am roughly shutting off this subject, and I hope you will be able to talk about it next time as freely as you would today."

However, there are occasions when a patient will not be able to talk freely at a later time if a subject is shunted aside at the particular moment that he has both the capacity and the special urgency to discuss it; an important therapeutic opportunity is lost for a long time, or perhaps permanently. There are, nevertheless, ways in which a therapist can organize his schedule to permit the kind of flexibility Sullivan advocates. If a therapist leaves open an hour late in each day's schedule he can make up the extra time and end his day's work at his usual hour. If none of his patients needs extra time on any particular day, the vacant hour can be used for dictating notes, doing minor paperwork, returning telephone calls and taking care of other such obligations.

The payment for extra time is a sticky matter; the manner in which a therapist handles it depends of whether he feels he is renting time to patients or giving them an interpersonal service. Whatever his point of view, it should at some point be defined. "I do not charge extra when we occasionally run over the allotted time because we are discussing something of special urgency. This is my policy with all my patients." "When we spend extra time working on your problems, it is only reasonable that the fee reflects this increase. This is my policy with all my patients, and it is the accepted practice in this kind of work." It is important that the therapist, as in these two quotations, indicates that whatever he does is in keeping with his standard policy; he is not doing the patient a special favor if he does not charge, nor is he penalizing the patient as a special case if he does charge. Failure to make this point clear in a tactful manner may lead an occasional patient to feel that the therapist has a particular personal interest in him if he gives extra time and does not charge, or that he is acting in a callous or punitive way if he does charge. The therapist must, of course, use good clinical judgment in deciding what is urgent material that may be allowed to override the clock, and what is clinging dependence, or mere garrulousness or some other activity that unjustifiably tends to stretch out the session.

There are other harmful topics of a more elusive nature. At times a therapist must be careful not to enter areas into which the patient cannot accompany him. The therapist sometimes should recognize that there are age differences, or educational gaps or socioeconomic dissimilarities between him and some patients that can cause therapeutic difficulties; he should not broach topics, or use words, or assume funds of knowledge and experience which are unfamiliar to his patients. For example, if in a question or a comment the therapist refers to the patient's vacation plans or recreational activities in a way that ignores the patient's economic limitations, the patient may feel humiliated or resentful. More often, however, he senses a gap in experience between himself and the therapist which discourages him from feeling that the therapist can truly understand his problems.

A therapist occasionally may feel that he should prevent a patient from discussing a subject which will be too upsetting for him to handle. The therapist at such times should be careful to avoid actions which make the patient feel censured or rejected, or which lead him to feel that the therapist is insensitive to his needs. The therapist should, after getting a limited amount of information on the potentially harmful topic, direct the interview into another area. For example, he may say, "Well, this leads us to consider such and such," or "There is another aspect of this that we perhaps should take a look at. How do you and your marital partner get along in this regard?" Nonverbal measures, such as a shift of body posture, or an alteration of voice tone or a change of facial expression, often smooth a move away from a topic which the therapist fears will mobilize panic, or profound feelings of inadequacy or other untoward reactions in the patient.

A therapist on occasion must prevent interview time from being spent in discussions of religious, or philosophical or moral issues. After listening to the patient talk about one of these subjects for a brief time, the therapist should indicate tactfully that these things lie outside the scope of the psychotherapeutic work in which he and the patient are engaged.

These are not *interpersonal issues* (at least in the usual psychiatric sense of the term). The therapist may say, "These subjects are important to many people; they cover many aspects of the meaning and significance of life. However, our job here is to deal with the interpersonal and emotional difficulties in your life. Nevertheless, some patients discover that after they have solved some of their interpersonal and emotional turmoil in psychotherapy they can settle religious [or philosophical or moral] issues which troubled them." In this way the therapist does not deprecate the patient's religious or moral quandaries; he recognizes their importance but indicates they are outside his field of expertise.

Regardless of precautions the therapist takes, panic is sometimes precipitated during an interview; as outlined in Chapter 3, panic paralyzes a therapeutic session and at times threatens the continuity of therapy. Hence, the therapist should take immediate, forceful steps. He may intervene and say, "Is this subject really so pressing right now? Can we set it aside for a while?" "We don't actually know much about this other individual yet. What could we get out of discussing your relationship with him right now?" Other examples are given in the discussion of *abrupt transitions* in Chapter 8. Questions, such as those employed in the two examples above, often are more effective than statements in a crisis of this kind. The questions, or statements, should by their wording suggest that the panic-ridden topic is not being permanently put aside, but is merely being shelved until it can be comfortably handled.

In a case of full-fledged panic the therapist may do further things to change the pace and focus of the interview. Sullivan recommends that when panic erupts in a schizoid or frankly schizophrenic patient the therapist may say, "Things are getting pretty tense; let's take a break for a few minutes and let things settle down," and then stretch, get up and walk about the room a bit. The patient may be invited to follow suit, and the therapist may add, "We're between innings now; we're taking a break for a few minutes." Reassuring, calming vocal inflections and other nonverbal accompaniments are important in the success of such measures to reduce panic.

If weeks or months later the therapist feels the patient can deal comfortably with a previously avoided harmful topic, he may approach it again. "Some time ago, while discussing your relationship with your parents, you mentioned such and such. However, at the time it seemed a pretty tense thing to go into. Perhaps the time has come when we can discuss it more comfortably." "Earlier in treatment we touched on that issue but did not feel it was a good time to go into it in detail. Now I think can we can see it in a wider context, and can deal with it."

3. THE HANDLING OF JARGON

Sullivan feels that many words have been so loosely and promiscuously employed in talking about psychotherapy that they have become part of a psychiatric jargon that at times is an obstacle in doing therapy. In many cases it is not clear what either a patient or a therapist means when he uses terms such as "repress," "hostility," "fixation" and many others.

The therapist and the patient must go behind these words and find out *what actually is happening in the patient's life.*

Patient: My sister often was very *aggressive* toward me as we were growing up.

Therapist: Can you tell me about some incidents in which she was *aggressive* toward you?

Patient: Well, whenever I did anything that I thought was pretty good, she went out of her way to criticize it, or she made fun of it, or she ran it down in some way.

Therapist: In other words, part of her aggressiveness consisted of trying to humiliate you and make you feel worthless.

Patient: Yes. Besides that, she boasted about anything she could do that I couldn't. For instance, she was good at sports, and I wasn't, and she harped on it all the time.

In this abbreviated dialogue the therapist and the patient are discovering that the patient uses the word *aggressiveness* (a term so loosely employed in many instances that it has acquired the characteristics of jargon) to designate things that often are not meant by it. The patient employs this word to cover a wide variety of her sister's harsh acts and attitudes toward her. If the therapist had accepted the term *aggressiveness* at face value and had not investigated it in detail, he would not have understood what the patient was talking about. Much important material would have remained unexplored and, worse still, the therapist probably would have *misunderstood* what happened in the patient's life.

Sullivan feels that terms such as *psychosis, neurosis, complex* and many others often hide more than they reveal about patients. If a patient brings up one of these terms, the therapist may say, "I really don't know what *psychosis* means, but perhaps we can find out what you were so frightened and perplexed about." "People mean many different things when they talk about *neurosis*. I think we shall understand your difficulties better if we explore the troubling things that have happened to you and the impacts they have had on you."

4. THE PRINCIPLE OF RECIPROCAL EMOTIONS AND ITS RELATION TO THERAPEUTIC DIFFICULTIES

Sullivan feels that each interpersonal relationship proceeds according to a set of rules which he terms *the principle of reciprocal emotions*. This principle states that in *every* two-person relationship

(1) the *needs* of each person are met or not met,

(2) the *interpersonal patterns* between the two persons evolve in healthy or unhealthy ways, and

(3) each person forms *expectations of satisfaction or non-fulfillment of his future needs* in this relationship.

In more complex ways this principle also operates in relationships involving more than two persons. However, we are interested only in those aspects of it which apply to the two-person relationship that occurs in psychotherapy.

The principle of reciprocal emotions operates to some extent in each patient-therapist relationship, and it may function in favorable or unfavorable ways. It is convenient to divide this subject into considering (1) the *needs* of the patient and the therapist, (2) the *interpersonal patterns* that arise between them and (3) the *expectations of how future needs* will be satisfied or thwarted in each of them.

Needs

The patient obviously has strong needs, though he may not understand them; if he did not have some special needs he would not be in therapy. His overall need is improvement of his interpersonal and emotional functioning to achieve more effective, comfortable ways of living.

The needs of the therapist are less obvious. As a rule, however, he has a need to feel that he is a useful person who is helping the patient to work on his difficulties; he has a need to maintain his self-esteem as a reasonably competent professional person. Any other needs which the therapist has in the patient-therapist relationship should be minimal if he is to function well in his task.

Interpersonal Patterns

If the patient-therapist interaction develops in satisfactory ways the patient feels that his treatment needs are being met, and the therapist's need to feel he is a competent professional person also is satisfied. If, on the other hand, the patterns of interaction develop in unsatisfactory ways because of inexperience or errors of the therapist, or because of intransigent personality traits in the patient, the patient may become anxious, or demoralized or upset in some other manner. His needs for therapeutic benefit are not met; in addition, the therapist may be defeated in his needs to feel reasonable self-esteem in his work.

Expectations of How Future Needs Will Be Met

Based on the two preceding sets of factors, the patient and the therapist will feel hopeful, or discouraged, about the future of therapy and the benefit the patient may get from it. The patient, of course, has other specific problems for which he is seeking help. However, for purposes of clear exposition we are here concentrating only on this fundamental, overall need.

During the rest of this discussion we shall look at the principle of reciprocal emotions mainly from the viewpoint of the therapist. Let us assume that in a particular case the patient is not making progress in psychotherapy, and his needs for emotional and interpersonal improvement are not being met. As a result, the therapist's needs to feel that he is a helpful person with special skills are not being met.

It is important that this therapist understand what is going on and thus not develop reactions which damage his relationship with the patient. He should proceed to take inventory of the therapeutic situation to see if he can employ fresh methods to invigorate it. He should search for factors in himself, or in the patient, that are blocking progress. In some cases he may decide to review the case with a colleague to see what can be done. Regardless of the outcome of this survey, the therapist is acting in a healthy interpersonal manner *because he is not allowing the nonfulfillment of his needs to push him into attitudes and actions that harm the patient.*

In contrast, if the therapist does not understand how the principle of reciprocal emotions is operating in this situation, he may develop damaging attitudes toward the patient. Because the patient is not meeting his needs, he may develop feelings of boredom or thinly disguised irritability toward the patient. He may blame the patient for the unsatisfactory state of affairs. "The patient is not well motivated for treatment." "The patient has entrenched secondary gains from his symptoms which make him resist all therapeutic moves." "The patient refuses to become truly involved in the therapeutic process."

There may, of course, be some truth in these assertions. However, it is important that none of the therapist's attitudes be precipitated mainly by the patient's nonfulfillment of the therapist's needs. The therapist who remains aware of the continual operation of the principle of reciprocal emotions in psychotherapy can avoid these mistakes.

Out of the interaction of the needs of the patient and the needs of the therapist a constructive, therapeutic *interpersonal pattern*, or a harmful one, evolves. The nature of this pattern, moreover, determines their expectations of *future events*.

An inexperienced or inept therapist may at times have nontherapeutic needs in his relationship with the patient. For example, if the therapist has strong needs to impress the patient with his competence he may act in ways that convey the impression that he is a prominent or extraordinarily able person. This quickly distorts the patient-therapist relationship since many of the therapist's acts and words are designed to meet his own needs rather than the patient's. In time the patient may sense that something is wrong in therapy, though usually he cannot perceive the situation well enough to put it into words; he merely knows that he is not getting much out of treatment. He often abandons therapy, frequently with the feeling that in some vague way its failure was his fault.

In some cases, however, the patient, without being aware of it, slips into a pattern that meets nontherapeutic needs of the therapist. Thus, if the therapist has needs to feel that he is an authoritative person to whose superior insights others should defer, the patient becomes ingratiating. He talks on subjects that elicit encouraging comments from the therapist and avoids those facets of his life which the therapist feels are irrelevant; in this the patient is guided mainly by nonverbal clues in the therapist's behavior. In time, the patient speaks only about the areas of his experience which tend to confirm the therapist's theories about what is wrong with him, and he reflects viewpoints and attitudes which dovetail with the therapist's ideas about what should occur in therapy. When this happens, true therapy often stops, or at least its value is much diminished, though neither the patient nor the therapist may know it. The therapeutic situation is for the most part meeting the needs of a therapist *who does not recognize how the principle of reciprocal emotions is operating in a nontherapeutic manner.*

Each therapist from time to time should use the principle of reciprocal emotions to make sure that therapy is on its proper path; it can be a kind of compass which keeps therapy directed toward its valid goals.

5. SPECIAL CONSIDERATIONS IN MODIFIED, OR BRIEF, PSYCHOTHERAPY

In some of his teachings during the last years of his life Sullivan expresses the opinion that intensive, prolonged psychotherapy is technically and economically practical for only a minority of the persons in the general community who need psychotherapeutic help. Brief, modified courses of psychotherapy with limited goals constitute the only workable approach for many persons whom a therapist encounters. A decision about the kind of therapy a patient needs and is able to participate in can be made only after careful evaluation of him; this evaluation may require up to several interviews and in itself may, of course, have therapeutic value for an appreciable number of persons.

In brief psychotherapy the therapist as a rule establishes specific goals and circumscribed areas for consideration. He may, in essence, say, "I feel our best course is to work on your adjustment in your job situation. Your most stressful difficulties with people seem to be there. Our goal will be to achieve a better adjustment in that area of your life." The therapist may go on to say that investigation of other facets of the patient's life can be planned at a later time. He may suggest that this be done after a "vacation" from therapy or after a lapse of time in which the patient consolidates the gains he has made.

After careful evaluation of the patient's problems, the therapist in some cases may feel that the most he can offer is some direct advice. Counseling about a few features of the patient's life may be the only practical course. Thus, he may make some concrete suggestions about the patient's vocational, or social or family adjustment. Sullivan feels that this is one of the most difficult things in the whole range of mental health work; to do it in a sound manner the therapist must have a firm grasp of the patient's life situation, and he should make only those recommendations that the patient can accept and act upon with reasonable comfort. It is of no use to recommend things the patient is emotionally unable to do; such advice may in some instances make the patient feel even more inadequate and anxious than previously. (The subject of advice, especially as it applies to prolonged psychotherapy, is covered at greater length in Chapter 10.)

In some cases the therapist supports the patient in making moves which obviously are necessary for his welfare but which the patient fears to make without the aid of a professional person. The therapist may support the patient in leaving an intolerable job situation, in establishing a residence separate from that of his parents, in making decisions about educational plans, and in doing many other things. The therapist may say, "I think we can both see that this change is in your best interests. It is possible you already felt so before you came to see me, but needed to talk the problem over with a neutral, uninvolved professional person. It sometimes is useful to lay a matter of this sort out on the table and take an objective look at it with someone who has special experience in dealing with problems in living."

A therapist should, in general, be very cautious in giving advice concerning decisions to marry or divorce. He should emphasize that the decision must be the patient's; the therapist can do no more than examine the situation carefully with the patient and help him to see all facets of it. The central question is, is this mariage or divorce in the patient's best long-term emotional and interpersonal interests? The therapist may ask, "Do you know enough about this person to make a decision to marry at this time? Should you wait until your interpersonal relationship with him/her is sounder, or until you understand his/her personality better?" In the case of a divorce the therapist may ask, "Have you explored all reasonable avenues to a better marital relationship? What are your plans for your life after a divorce? In brief, will your emotional and interpersonal *needs* be best met by a divorce?"

Sullivan stresses that good brief psychotherapy depends on economical use of time, close attention to the problem at hand and avoidance of digressions. The therapist occasionally may have to ask in as tactful a manner as possible, "Is this relevant to the main problem we are working on? This undoubtedly is important to you, but perhaps we should keep our focus on the goals we set ourselves at the beginning."

In brief psychotherapy the assets and liabilities in the patient's total range of interpersonal activity are evaluated; the healthier parts of it often are mobilized to help the patient achieve a better adjustment. For example, a person who is experiencing much anxiousness and interpersonal stress in a job he cannot leave may be urged to get as much satisfaction as possible in his family life and in those social areas in which he has sound relationships, to counterbalance the grinding pressures in his work setting.

Sullivan points out that psychotherapy is, as treatment methods go, still in its early stages of evolution. A therapist must recognize what is practical in the case of each patient and attempt no more than he can reasonably hope to achieve. A therapist should not, either implicitly or explicitly, promise more than he can deliver. As a pragmatic clinician Sullivan emphasizes that a therapist deals with each patient *in the way that is most likely to work*. Theory, and even the treatment format itself, bow to the practical necessities of the patient. In brief psychotherapy, for instance, the therapist sometimes deliberately curbs a growth of awareness that would not be useful, and might even be upsetting, to the patient.

Patients who achieve fresh orientations and viewpoints in brief psychotherapy may make a good deal of progress in applying them in the many hours between therapeutic sessions, and accumulating benefits frequently do not cease with termination of treatment. They continue to accrue as the patient's capacities for better interpersonal relationships and more effective communication help him in his daily life; personality growth often acquires a certain momentum of its own.

Chapter 10

The Structuring of an Interview

A. THE BASIC FORMAT OF INTERVIEWING

Sullivan feels that each interview, or series of interviews, should have an underlying format of four general phases: (1) the *inception*, (2) the *reconnaissance*, (3) the *detailed inquiry* and (4) the *termination*.

These four stages are not rigidly employed. From the accounts of persons who were treated by Sullivan himself, he did not meticulously follow them. They are more a way of conceptualizing what occurs in psychotherapy than a rigidly prescribed manner of doing it. They constitute a way of looking at the data and organizing it, and of sketching a general approach to each problem the patient and the therapist consider.

Sullivan believes that these four phases can be employed to organize and view (1) an individual interview, (2) a course of psychotherapy, which may be brief or long, and (3) any particular facet of the patient's life, such as his marital adjustment or his relationship with his parents.

During most of the rest of this chapter we shall employ these terms (*inception, reconnaissance, detailed inquiry* and *termination*) *as they apply to a prolonged course of psycho-therapy*. However, their other usages should not be forgotten.

THE INCEPTION

We shall approach the *inception* by first discussing the details of the therapist's initial contact with the patient, and we shall then consider some of its more general aspects.

Sullivan recommends that the therapist learn the name of each new patient and greet him with it on their first contact; the patient's correct name, including its proper pronunciation in some cases, can be obtained by the therapist or by his receptionist from the individual (such as a referring professional person, or the patient himself or some other party) who makes the appointment. This may seem a trivial matter, but it mars the atmosphere somewhat to fumble over a patient's name or to mispronounce it. Sullivan's meticulousness on this point is characteristic of his continual emphasis that the interview is an *interpersonal* process in which all possible steps should be taken to support the patient's feelings of self-esteem and worthwhileness as a person; he is of sufficient consequence for the therapist to take the trouble to get his name right.

Sullivan as a rule sat about 10 feet in front of the patient and turned his body and gaze toward a point that was about 90 degrees to the patient's right or left. He felt that looking continuously at the patient made both the patient and the therapist uncomfortable; looking at a point somewhat to one side of the patient diminished this discomfort. It also allowed the therapist easily to turn his gaze toward the patient whenever he wished.

The amount of time a therapist employing this position looks to one side of the patient or straight at him varies much from one therapist to another, and is influenced by what is going on in the interviews. This flexible position permits the therapist to be alertly attentive to what the patient is saying and doing at almost all times since the patient is usually within the range of the peripheral vision of the therapist, and any sudden or marked movements are perceived.

At the beginning of the first interview the therapist should, at least briefly, tell the patient what he already knows about him. For example, the therapist might say, "Dr. Smith, as you know, called and set up this appointment for you. He said you have been feeling anxious lately and have been having some difficulties in your relationships with people. He indicated that you have tended to avoid people and have spent much time by yourself. He thought that perhaps you could benefit from seeing me about these problems. He did not tell me more than that; this is the limit of my information about you."

This sets the interview, or series of interviews, on a frank footing. It helps the patient feel that the therapist does not have preconceived opinions about him and clears the air for the patient and the therapist to define and explore his difficulties. It also gives the patient an opportunity to correct any information the therapist has. If the therapist has received a good deal of information, such as photocopies of reports from previous therapists (as a rule, of course, after the patient has given permission to the previous therapists or clinics), the therapist may summarize it in a few words and inquire if it is accurate. He may ask, "Is that more or less how you see the situation?" "Does this agree, on the whole, with how you view your reasons for coming to see me, and the general situation in your life?"

There are, however, some limiting factors in the amount of collateral information which the therapist reviews with the patient. Data which might be quite disturbing to the patient, or which might force him to become defensive, or which might cause him to abandon the evaluation at the end of the first session, may be withheld. Clinical judgment determines these matters.

For example, if the referring physician or other person states that in his opinion the patient is psychotic, or urgently needs psychiatric hospitalization, or is dangerous, the therapist probably will not reveal these opinions to the patient, but will assess the situation and come to his own conclusions. A therapist rarely should refuse to receive collateral information; it may be important, or even crucial. Thus, if the patient has made recent suicidal attempts, or is addicted to a narcotic, or has recently been psychiatrically hospitalized for a grave disorder, the therapist may need this information to make a sound evaluation of him, since some patients do not reveal such information or may even conceal it deliberately.

In many cases the therapist should get confirmation of collateral information from the patient during the first one or two interviews. He may do so *directly* by asking, "Have things recently seemed so hopeless that you have thought of harming yourself, or have even made attempts to do so?" "Have these problems at any time appeared so overwhelming that you have considered psychiatric hospitalization, or have actually had such help?" In other instances the therapist may seek confirmation of collateral data *indirectly*. For example, a careful examination of the patient's vocational history may reveal a time gap and thus lead to discussion of a recent psychiatric hospitalization. A checkered vocational career with many abrupt job changes may proceed easily into discussion of severe alcoholism, a problem which the patient at first minimized.

Note-taking is always a somewhat controversial subject. Sullivan almost routinely took notes during the first couple of interviews, or so, and then relegated note-taking to summaries written or dictated after each interview, or after several interviews during a morning's or afternoon's work.

During the initial interviews (as will be discussed in the section on the *reconnaissance*), the therapist as a rule is busy getting a bird's-eye view of who the patient is, what the general outline of his life has been, and why he has come to see the therapist. This involves a lot of factual data such as the patient's age, his marital status, the number of his siblings and his position among them, his parents' whereabouts and their current relationship with him, his educational background, his vocational status and similar information. Getting at least a brief sketch of such information enables the therapist to take a global look at the patient and decide what kind of therapy best meets his needs.

Sullivan feels that few therapists can get this information and record it accurately for future review without taking notes in the first two or three interviews. He recommends that the therapist explain this succinctly to the patient. "In the first couple of interviews, or so, we shall get an outline of a lot of things in your life. It is difficult for a therapist to keep in mind such things as how many brothers and sisters you have, and where you went to school and so forth unless he takes notes while these things are being surveyed. After the first few sessions I probably won't take notes during the interviews. We'll be far too busy for that."

Sullivan concedes that perhaps there are therapists who can take notes regularly during a course of psychotherapy without marring the patient-therapist relationship, but he feels such therapists are rare. If a therapist continues to take notes throughout psychotherapy, one of two things happens. Either the therapist's attention to his note-taking distracts him from what is going on between him and the patient and hinders the therapeutic relationship, or the notes are so hurriedly and poorly made that they are of little value.

Moreover, after the first few sessions, note-taking decreases the spontaneity of some patients. It smacks of a journalist-interviewee situation rather than a patient-therapist one; it may give the interview a cold, impersonal tone. It is difficult to be a vigilant, involved participant observer and take notes at the same time. With some types of patients the therapist should not take notes during the first few sessions. These patients include children, adolescents, paranoid persons, extremely upset individuals and some others; such persons often become guarded and uncommunicative if the therapist takes notes.

The therapist often begins the *inception* by inquiring about the difficulty which has caused the patient to seek help. "Perhaps you might begin by telling me about the kind of problem, or difficulty in living, that brings you to see me." The therapist's initial question or comment should be so broad that it essentially is no more than a general invitation to talk. If the patient is quite tense, the therapist may say, "Perhaps you might begin to talk about yourself in whatever way you feel is best and most comfortable. If you do that, we'll get to your problems in time." The response to such an invitation to talk can be led into definition of the reasons for seeking help, at least as they appear at the time to the patient; in time they merge imperceptibly into the *reconnaissance* and the *detailed inquiry*.

In the *inception*, an interpersonal relationship between the therapist and the patient is begun. In the *reconnaissance*, this interpersonal relationship is used to make a broad survey of the patient's life situation and difficulties.

Throughout these discussions of the inception, the reconnaissance, the detailed inquiry and the termination, we are covering only basic features and points that are likely to be of special interest or practical usefulness for therapists. An exhaustive survey of Sullivan's four-part schema would require a large amount of space, would contain many things that are common knowledge among almost all therapists, and would repeat a large part of the material discussed in earlier chapters of this book. In addition, a meticulous inventory of these four stages would tend to negate the fundamental principle that they constitute a way of looking at data about patients rather than a rigidly prescribed way of getting it.

THE RECONNAISSANCE

In the reconnaissance, the patient and the therapist take a broad look at the patient's life. Although this survey often has therapeutic value for the patient in itself, its main aim is to establish *a general outline of who the patient is and the experiences which have molded his personality and problems.*

A reconnaissance may take from one to a dozen or more interviews; it usually occupies several sessions. At its end (and here the features of the *reconnaissance* and the *termination* overlap and blend into each other to some extent), the therapist summarizes what he and the patient have learned, and they make plans for further treatment, such as individual psychotherapy, or group psychotherapy or some other kind of treatment experience. When systematic treatment follows the reconnaissance, the interviews pass into the phase of the *detailed inquiry*.

For the sake of clarity, the distinction between the reconnaissance and the detailed inquiry should be emphasized at this point. The reconnaissance (the term *general survey* might be considered a synonym of it) is a broad inventory of the patient's past and current life with incidental, limited therapeutic aspects, and the detailed inquiry is an extensive, exploratory course of psychotherapy whose main aim is therapeutic.

Sullivan feels that in order to carry out effective treatment the therapist must have at his disposal the sketch of the patient's life history and current adjustment which is elicited in the reconnaissance. This information allows him to put into perspective all things that come later. The therapist is able to help the patient to make connections and to see the relevance of one event in his life to another.

At the beginning, the patient is a *stranger,* but during the reconnaissance he gradually takes form as a *person* with whom the therapist can go on to do effective work. If a *stranger* tells something about his life, it is difficult to know what to make of it, for it cannot be linked to anything else in his present or past. If, however, a known *person* tells something about himself, one can evaluate its importance or triviality and see where it fits into his total life picture.

In his lectures and seminars Sullivan outlines an extensive scheme for carrying out the reconnaissance. It embraces an examination of the patient's childhood relationships with his parents and siblings, his grade school and high school adjustments, his childhood and adolescent experiences in various social areas, his later educational experiences, his vocational history, his sexual adjustment, his adult social activities, his cultural and avocational interests, his personal habits, and many other facets of his life. In all areas the emphasis is on *interpersonal* and *emotional* aspects.

During the reconnaissance *the therapist employs many of the techniques of interviewing discussed in the preceding chapters of this book.* For example, he notes that inquiry into particular subjects makes the patient increasingly anxious and he shifts attention to other regions of the patient's life so that marked anxiety, or even panic, may not become an obstructing force in the exploratory process. He notes these anxiety-laden areas for later, gradual examination if the patient enters into prolonged therapy at the conclusion of the reconnaissance. During the reconnaissance the therapist tends to ask broad questions that invite the patient to talk as spontaneously as possible about particular aspects of his life. More extensive investigations are reserved for the detailed inquiry.

In addition to getting a general view of the patient's past and current life experiences, the therapist also notes during the reconnaissance the patient's reactions in the interview situation. These include his emotional reactions to the things he talks about and the kind of interpersonal relationship he tends to set up with the therapist. The therapist observes the patient's capacity to communicate, his emotional responsiveness, his ability to grasp and understand new things, his rigidity or flexibility in dealing with the therapist, and his tendencies to be controlling, suspicious, reserved, passive, hostile, contemptuous, apologetic, evasive and manipulating. These are only a few of the things the therapist makes note of. In all these things the emphasis is on what occurs between the patient and the people around him and between the patient and the therapist.

Sullivan feels that a completed reconnaissance is essential for making therapeutic plans. Only after he has a broad overview of the patient and his problems can the therapist make plans for formal psychotherapy or recommend some other kind of help. A therapist should not agree to begin prolonged, intensive psychotherapy if he lacks the information to determine whether such treatment has a reasonably good chance of helping the patient.

At the end of the reconnaissance the therapist usually summarizes his impressions; as noted above, here the reconnaissance and some aspects of the termination coincide and merge. The therapist lays out somewhat systematically what he and the patient have established about the patient's problems and interpersonal patterns. During this summary he offers the patient ample opportunities to amend and comment on his formulations. This particular part of the reconnaissance may have significant therapeutic value for some patients, though that is not its primary aim.

The therapist then recommends whatever kind of treatment, or other steps, he feels will best help the patient. He may recommend individual extensive psychotherapy, either with himself or with some other therapist, or he may suggest a course of brief, modified psychotherapy. He may propose group psychotherapy, or family therapy, or individual or joint marital counseling, or some other special form of treatment. In some cases he may make concrete recommendations about changes in the patient's life situation.

At the conclusion of the reconnaissance the interview process passes into the phase of either the detailed inquiry or the termination, depending on the therapist's conclusions and the kinds of recommendations he makes to the patient.

THE DETAILED INQUIRY

The detailed inquiry is an exploration in depth of the patient's life and problems. *It covers what, in general, constitutes the main body of a course of psychotherapy.*

The things that occur during the detailed inquiry have been discussed at length in the preceding chapters of this book. In the detailed inquiry the patient's anxieties, security operations, self-system, dynamisms, parataxic distortions, and other personality features are explored. A broad spectrum of his interpersonal and emotional functioning is investigated, and consensual validation is gradually achieved in many areas.

In this work Sullivan recommends as a basic format his concept of personality evolution through a series of developmental stages; they are (1) infancy, (2) childhood, (3) the juvenile period, (4) preadolescence, (5) early adolescence, (6) late adolescence and its termination in (7) adulthood.

Two things are noteworthy in this scheme of development. First, the dividing lines between these stages are always determined by interpersonal factors. Thus, infancy ends and childhood begins when the person begins to develop articulate speech (an interpersonal tool). Childhood ends when the person acquires a need for association with nonfamily children of his own age group. Second, Sullivan places more emphasis on adolescence as a period of continuous personality growth than many other psychiatric authorities.

Although psychotherapy varies much in content from one patient to the next, in a sizable number of cases a large part of the detailed inquiry is spent exploring childhood and adolescent experiences. They are not examined as ends in themselves but with the intention of showing *how interpersonal patterns were laid down in the patient's personality structure during his formative years and still operate in his current dealings with people. Sullivan feels that, in this respect, the purpose of therapy is not to extirpate* (that is, eradicate or uproot) *old interpersonal traumas from childhood and adolescence by talking about them, but to bring their many facets fully into comfortable awareness and to link these traumas up with current, day-to-day interpersonal and emotional functioning.* Many examples of this have been given in the early chapters of this book.

This is a major part of the business of the detailed inquiry. *The patient and the therapist explore how current interpersonal problems are continuations of warped ways of interacting with people that began in unhealthy relationships in the patient's formative years.*

It is beyond the scope of this book, which is devoted to Sullivan's therapeutic techniques, to cover in detail his scheme of personality development. This would require a great deal of space and is peripheral to our main concerns here. The reader who wishes to become familiar with this subject can do so by consulting the relevant material in Sullivan's works, which are listed and described in detail in the second half of Chapter 11.

The detailed inquiry varies much in length. In brief, modified psychotherapy it may last from a dozen sessions to many more. In intensive, prolonged psychotherapy it may occupy up to hundreds of interviews. Sullivan notes that the benefits of psychotherapy are not necessarily proportional to its length. Many other variables affect how beneficial it is in any particular case. Skillfully conducted brief, modified psychotherapy may in many cases accomplish more than prolonged therapy. Treatment is molded to fit the patient's needs, and meeting those needs requires that the therapist be willing to be flexible.

THE TERMINATION

Sullivan uses the word *termination* in three different ways. He employs it to designate (1) the final minutes of every interview, (2) the end of the reconnaissance and the formulations given the patient at that time and (3) the final steps in ending a course of systematic psychotherapy. As noted earlier, in some cases there is a certain amount of overlapping of these three usages of this word.

The Termination of Each Interview

Regardless of where an interview occurs in any kind of patient-therapist contact, Sullivan feels the therapist should give a brief summary, or recapitulation, of whatever has been accomplished; in some instances, however, the therapist merely selects for the termination some aspect of the interview which he considers important and comments on it. As a rule this occurs during the last minute or two of the interview and usually can be done in half a dozen concise sentences.

Sullivan holds that a patient should carry away something beneficial from each interview. He feels this is a practical necessity in therapy, in addition to being in the patient's best interests, and that patients more or less expect it in our culture. A patient may take away a new viewpoint about some facet of his experience, or a feeling that is better crystallized in words, or some new insight about his ways of relating with people. The patient's gain may be a state of less anxiety and increased emotional security about some aspect of his life. Whatever its nature, the encapsulation of this gain in a brief summary should occur at the end of *all* interviews, regardless of the nature of the session or the stage of therapy.

For example, toward the end of an interview a therapist may say, "Today we've talked about your fears that people will retaliate against you in various ways if you are at all assertive. We have seen that you fear that if you are assertive others will not like you, will withhold their affection from you, will withdraw from you, and will leave you in isolation. I think we shall find, as you experiment with assertiveness in your day-to-day life, that these feared things do not occur. We can work much more on this in future sessions."

Here, in terminating, the therapist has given the patient a clear summary of what went on in the interview, and he has indicated that working on the problem offers opportunities for progress.

When the purposes of treatment are limited, as in modified, brief psychotherapy, the therapist may offer advice. This frequently is put in the form of a challenging question. "Have you ever considered discussing this frankly with your marital partner?" "Have you ever experimented with being more assertive and holding your ground on some of these issues?" "When you became involved in affectionate relationships in the past, did they lead to disasters? Does it seem likely that would happen in this relationship?" The general subject of advice is discussed further in the final section of this chapter.

At its end an interview should not be simply chopped off by announcing that the patient's time is up. Many therapists lose much that they gain in an interview by the manner in which they end it. The "Well, that's it for today" atmosphere in which many hours end casts a cold feeling over the entire session. It smacks of abrupt rejection once the time for which the patient pays has expired. The patient should leave with the feeling that he and the therapist accomplished something, however small; he should feel that each interview is a worthwhile experience. The therapist's final words, encapsulating something that was accomplished in the interview, achieve this.

In taking leave of the patient, the therapist should employ an expression that links the current session to the next one. For example, the therapist may say, "I think we must stop now and go on next time." In place of an abrupt "good-bye," the therapist's final words may be, "Good-bye, for now," or "Until our next session, good-bye." These, and similar, expressions bridge the present to the future and emphasize the continuity of therapy.

The Termination of a Reconnaissance or of a Course of Psychotherapy

As noted at the beginning of this section, Sullivan also employs the word *termination* to designate the summary or formulation given the patient at the end of a reconnaissance or in the final phase of a systematic course of psychotherapy. We shall turn our attention to these two other types of termination.

The therapist may spend from several minutes to up to half a session or so in summarizing what he and the patient have accomplished during a reconnaissance; he may spend similar periods of time in crystallizing what has been achieved in a brief, modified course of therapy or a prolonged course of psychotherapy. This subject has been discussed to some extent in the section on the reconnaissance earlier in this chapter.

During the termination the therapist offers the patient opportunities to amend the things he says, and he and the patient may discuss the patient's comments and views. *The summary thus is a dialogue* and not a lecture by the therapist; it is a give-and-take process in which both the therapist and the patient participate.

In a terminal formulation at the end of psychotherapy, the therapist may cover many things. He may recapitulate some of the aspects of the patient's interpersonal and emotional life that have become clear during therapy. He may outline some of the distortions in the patient's associations with people that have manifested themselves both in the things the patient talked about and in his relationship with the therapist. Problems which the patient formerly camouflaged with rationalizations and clichés may be concisely reviewed. The terminal formulation may deal with anxieties and security operations that have been elucidated and unhealthy dynamisms that have been explored. A backward glance may be given to parataxic distortions that emerged and were resolved during therapy. In brief, the final formulation may deal with whatever aspects of therapy should be emphasized. In a sense, the terminal phase may take a bird's eye view of what happened in treatment, and it thus puts the whole therapeutic process in perspective.

Sullivan feels that many therapists underestimate the value of this kind of formulation at the end of reconnaissance, or at the conclusion of short or prolonged psychotherapy, or at various critical points in an extensive course of therapy. The summary often puts the therapeutic gains in a new light which enables a patient to see his total situation in a fresh manner. This may enable him to go forward in constructive, healthy ways.

B. MISCELLANEOUS ASPECTS OF INTERVIEWS

SEXUALITY, LUST AND INTIMACY

Sullivan does not attribute much importance to infantile and childhood sexuality in his concepts of personality development. He recognizes that rudimentary genital arousal may occur in infants and children, but he feels it does not play a major role in their interpersonal relationships and emotional functioning. In this matter his position obviously differs much from that of Freudian psychoanalysis.

To demarcate clearly his concept of the role of genital sexuality in interpersonal life, Sullivan employs the term lust. Sullivan lived and worked in psychiatric circles in which Freudian ideas were prevalent, and he needed another word than sexuality to make explicit the ways in which his concepts differed from those of Freud. If he had used sexuality and lust as synonyms, it would have confused many of his students, colleagues and readers.

Lust denotes all emotional forces which have genital sexual activity as their immediate or possible goal. The phrase *genital sexual activity* embraces all actions in which the genitals of one or two persons are involved; it thus includes masturbation and all kinds of genital activity between persons of the same or opposite sexes. The phrase *immediate or possible goal* indicates a spectrum of activity that ranges from genital-to-genital sexual intercourse to erotic daydreaming about a television or motion picture star.

Sullivan feels that lust does not become a major force in personality development until puberty begins to usher in physical sexual maturation between the ages of about 11 and 13. From that point onward, lust is a strong factor in interpersonal life. It draws people toward each other, and the individual's pattern of lust (heterosexual, homosexual or other) is a powerful influence in molding his way of life.

Sullivan feels that merely discussing what a person physically does with his lust, and how many times a week, is not a profitable way to study interpersonal problems. The therapist and the patient must go beyond the physical aspects of sexual expression and find out *what sexual expression means interpersonally and emotionally to a person*. How much true affection is involved in it? Is the patient's sexual activity mainly a physiological release, or does it occur in the context of an emotionally significant interpersonal situation? What, in brief, does this lustful relationship mean to the person, and how do other features of his interpersonal life dovetail with it? Is it an integrating force that draws two people together? Is lust operating in satisfying, healthy ways, or is it operating in sick, unsatisfactory ways?

Intimacy, both as a term and a concept, is important in Sullivan's interpersonal psychology. *Intimacy occurs when a person feels that the welfare of another individual is as important to him as his own well-being*. Intimacy is, in its way, as strong a force as lust, *but lust and intimacy are separate drives*.

Intimacy first appears in the strong, friendly relationships persons of the same sex have with each other in preadolescence; between the ages of about 8 and 11 boys have strong needs for friendly intimacy with other boys, and girls have similar feelings toward girls. Desirably, intimate drives in the preadolescent period *are not contaminated by lust*. With the onset of adolescence between the ages of 11 and 13, the drives toward intimacy and lust unite and turn toward persons of the opposite sex. Since both intimacy and lust have strong capacities to bind people together, this union produces a powerful interpersonal integrating force during the rest of life.

Discussion of what occurs in a person's intimate relationships with close friends, lovers, marital partners and others is a productive field for psychotherapeutic inquiry. The patient and the therapist can examine both the healthy and unhealthy features of intimate relationships. Because of their intensity, intimate relationships are fruitful areas for emotional development, for when two persons share and compare experiences in an intimate relationship they foster each other's personality growth; this is particularly so from early adolescence onward. The individual improves his capacities for close relationships with people in many facets of his life as a result of the special development that occurs in his intimate relationships.

Discussion of the problems a person has in his intimate relationships is often a revealing field for therapeutic work. The patient and the therapist can trace how the interpersonal traumas of childhood have left the patient ill equipped for sound intimate associations; in some cases interpersonal damage during adolescence further deforms his interpersonal abilities. Much psychotherapeutic work can be done by exploring how these traumas have hampered the person's capacities for intimacy in later life. Freeing the individual from inhibitions and distorted ways of interacting with people allows him to participate in healthy intimate relationships.

As two close persons exchange feelings and ideas and learn to adjust to each other, they automatically may improve personality problems they brought out of their formative years. Parataxic distortions of minor or moderate intensity may be corrected in the healthy interactions of a prolonged intimate interaction; even severe parataxic distortions may be improved to a limited extent. Similarly, troubling anxieties and sick security operations may be ameliorated. All these processes can be discussed during psychotherapy.

In addition, much healthy consensual validation usually

occurs in intimate relationships; they offer special opportunities for this.

Patient: Bob and I have a special closeness I've not known before. We can talk about what bothers each of us and what we like. We can talk over our differences and work out our problems.

Therapist: Could you do this with your parents?

Patient: No, there never seemed to be time, which I guess means I never had the kind of closeness with them that I have with Bob. My parents and I couldn't talk on the same level; they didn't seem to get the point when I tried to talk about any problems that occurred between them and me. We couldn't settle anything that really mattered.

Therapist: Were your parents close to each other?

Patient: I don't know, but I think not. At least, I never saw much closeness between them. If they had it, I wasn't aware of it.

Therapist: It seems the strong, warm intimacy you have with Bob is a healthy force in your life. In it you are developing new interpersonal strengths. You are growing in your capacities for relating warmly and smoothly with another person. In time this will affect your feelings about people in general and your relationships with them.

Exploring what goes on in sound, as well as troubled, intimate relationships can be important in psychotherapy.

HANDLING PATIENTS' UNREALISTIC EXPECTATIONS OF THERAPISTS

When Sullivan speaks of the *unrealistic expectations of therapists* which some patients develop in intensive, prolonged psychotherapy, he is referring to wishes to transform the therapeutic relationship into a sexual one or into a warm friendship. Sullivan's views on the nature of such feelings in patients are quite different from those of Freud.

Sullivan believes that the feelings which in Freudian psychoanalysis are termed *erotic transference* can be prevented by continual emphasis on the patient-therapist interaction as a work relationship for solving the interpersonal and emotional problems of the patient. Early in the course of treatment and occasionally thereafter, the therapist defines his role as that of a person who has special training and knowledge in interpersonal problems, and he specifies the patient's role as that of an individual who needs this kind of help.

The therapist thus may from time to time state, in essence, "Our job is to deal with your problems in living. You come here to work on these difficulties, and my task is to help you solve them by means of special knowledge and expertise." *Sullivan feels that erotic transference feelings can in the vast majority of cases be avoided by continual emphasis on the work the patient and the therapist are doing in a client-therapist relationship.*

Sullivan believes that erotic transference states develop when the patient-therapist interaction is not, both explicitly and implicitly, defined as a *client-expert work relationship*. When this is not repeatedly made clear, and confirmed by the therapist's behavior, a vacuum occurs in the patient-therapist situation, and the patient may gradually fill this vacuum with erotic feelings toward the therapist or feelings of admiration coupled with a desire for close friendship.

The therapist's theme is, "The important thing is the *work* we are doing. Though it must, of course, be carried out in the context of an expert-client relationship, the work is always our main concern." Sullivan states that in his many years of doing psychotherapy he rarely had significant difficulties with erotic feelings of patients toward him when he carefully defined the patient-therapist relationship in this manner.

The therapist's definition of his role must, of course, be confirmed by his behavior in the interviews. He should at all times, by his words and actions as an alert participant observer, be perceived by the patient as a professionally understanding and helpful person, and nothing more.

Sullivan views erotic feelings and expectations of a patient toward a therapist as contaminants of therapy. When a therapist allows them to flourish, they impair, or even destroy, treatment. The patient's feelings have transformed the *work* situation of therapy into a *personal, social* one in which true treatment cannot continue. The new patient-therapist relationship may gratify the patient; he may proclaim it to be beneficial to him because of his admiration for the therapist and attachment to him. However, the patient-therapist relationship has in fact become so distorted that effective psychotherapeutic work is impossible.

Sullivan's viewpoints on this subject often appear so novel to mental health professional persons trained in Freudian and Neo-Freudian points of view that their initial reaction is to dismiss them out of hand. However, when Sullivan's views are carefully studied from an objective point of view, and when his techniques for avoiding erotic feelings in patients are scrupulously employed, their validity and usefulness are readily demonstrated. I have rarely found them lacking in nearly 30 years of doing interpersonal psychotherapy.

Sullivan feels that the erotic feelings that often arise in Freudian psychoanalysis and some of its variants are products of the unusual nature of the patient-therapist relationship in those forms of therapy. A vacuum is created because the therapist does not clearly and repeatedly define the *working* nature of the patient-therapist relationship. The patient spends large amounts of time with the therapist discussing intimate aspects of his life in uninhibited ways. In this unique kind of experience the therapist never censures the patient and never